THE
WISDOM
OF
Baltasar
Gracián

◆

A PRACTICAL MANUAL
FOR GOOD
AND PERILOUS TIMES

THE
WISDOM
OF
Baltasar
Gracián

◆

A PRACTICAL MANUAL
FOR GOOD
AND PERILOUS TIMES

ADAPTED AND EDITED BY
J. Leonard Kaye

POCKET BOOKS

New York   London   Toronto   Sydney   Tokyo   Singapore

An *Original* Publication of POCKET BOOKS

POCKET BOOKS, a division of Simon & Schuster Inc.
1230 Avenue of the Americas, New York, NY 10020

ISBN: 0-671-79659-3

First Pocket Books trade paperback printing December 1992

10 9 8 7 6 5 4 3 2 1

POCKET and colophon are registered trademarks of
Simon & Schuster Inc.

Text and cover design by Stanley S. Drate/Folio Graphics Co. Inc.

Printed in the U.S.A.

Aphorisms are adapted from *A Truthtelling Manual and the Art of Wordly
Wisdom: Being a collection of the aphorisms which appear in the works of
Baltasar Gracián, immediately translated for the understanding from a 1653
Spanish Text* by Martin Fisher.

♦ ♦ ♦ ♦ ♦

*Dedicated to the memory of
my wonderful friend Joe Benaron,
whose earthly contributions
exceeded human expectations.*

♦ ♦ ♦ ♦ ♦

AUTHOR'S NOTE

✦ ✦ ✦ ✦ ✦

The complexity of meaning and multiple subject matter contained in some of Gracián's original aphorisms suggested that they be divided into separate sayings and be given new titles. This was done lovingly. There are also additional aphorisms contained in Gracián's completed *Oracle*.

I wish to express my warm gratitude to other devotees, writers, and researchers, near and far, who love Father Baltasar Gracián as I do. The following is a partial list of works that inspired me.

Baltasar Gracián: escritor aragones del siglo XVII, authored by Universidad de Zaragoza, 1926.

Gracián y el barroco by Miguel Batllori, Roma, Edizioni de Storia e Letteratura, 1958.

Baltasar Gracián by Virginia Ramos Foster, Phoenix College, © 1957 G. K. Hall & Co.

Homenaje a Gracián, por Ch. V. Aubrun. 1958 Zaragoza, Institucion "Fernando el Catolico."

ACKNOWLEDGMENTS

✦ ✦ ✦ ✦ ✦

Every work that reaches print is touched by a myriad of minds. I want to express my deepest gratitude to the people who contributed to this moment: C. J. A. for the greatest gift, the book; Midge Peltier for caring about every word; Warren Bayless for undangling the participles; Charles Slaughter for his tireless nagging and brutal criticism; Father Larry Battles, historian, for his ecumenical scrutiny; Dr. Charles Kelman for his personal interest; Philip Springer for early critical response; Betty Jurus and Maureen Daly for subsequent critical response; Elaine Pfefferblit for final encouragement; Jean Graham-Jones for her Spanish translations; Brent Sverdloff for research assistance; and my devoted wife, Lillian, mother of Richard, Barbara, and Ronnie, for deflecting burdens so that I could respond to the creative spark and spiritual fire.

Addendum: Born lucky is the writer who falls into *intelligent* hands. Thank you, Judith Regan, Simon & Schuster Senior Editor and VP.

J. L. K.

Rarely in the scale of fortune
Stands the fickle tongue at rest.
You must rise or you must sink,
Must be ruler and the winner,
Or be slave and be the loser,
Suffer or emerge triumphant,
Be the blade or be the block.

—*Goethe*

CONTENTS

GRACIÁN'S RECOLLECTIONS

✦

**The Second Entry:
MY EARLY YEARS**

THE ORACLE
Gracián On: Personal Behavior

✦ ✦ ✦

GRACIÁN'S RECOLLECTIONS
✦
The Third Entry:
MY DAYS AS A NOVICE

THE ORACLE
Gracián On: A Way Of Life

GRACIÁN'S RECOLLECTIONS

✦

**The Fourth Entry:
MY PROFESSORSHIP**

THE ORACLE
Gracián On: Friends, Rivals, and Enemies

GRACIÁN'S RECOLLECTIONS

✦

The Fifth Entry:
MY FIRST PUBLISHED BOOKS

THE ORACLE
Gracián On: Lessons and Warnings

GRACIÁN'S RECOLLECTIONS

✦

**The Sixth Entry:
REWARDS OF MATURITY**

THE ORACLE
Gracián On: Common Sense Decisions

GRACIÁN'S RECOLLECTIONS

✦

The Seventh Entry:
THE WRITING COMES OF AGE

THE ORACLE
Gracián On: Wise Men and Fools

GRACIÁN'S RECOLLECTIONS

◆

**The Eighth Entry:
THE SPANISH MIND**

THE ORACLE
Gracián On: Balance and Awareness

GRACIÁN'S RECOLLECTIONS

✦

The Ninth Entry:
THE LATE EVENING OF MY LIFE

THE ORACLE
Gracián On: Winning Ways

✦ ✦ ✦

PREFACE

Gracián:
The Rediscovery of a Genius

He counseled kings. His books were translated into every language in the civilized world. The greatest minds of Europe—Friedrich Nietzsche and Arthur Schopenhauer—drew inspiration from his writings. He was considered the genius of his age, yet the name Baltasar Gracián is unknown to all but a select few.

In presenting Gracián's illumination of old wisdom for the modern reader, I have a dual purpose. The first and foremost is to pay tribute to this Spanish Jesuit, who died in 1658 at the age of fifty-seven; the second is to provide individuals with an enlightened way to deal in all the arenas of their lives—business, political, and social.

Gracián's visionary words touch our minds and spirits, but they are not of a religious bent. Rather, his common sense material deals with men and women engaged in the business of living in a highly charged, aggressive era. His observations force us to examine our assets *and* our limitations. He helps us solve the many puzzles of life.

Gracián's seventeenth-century world of corruption, poverty, hypocrisy, and widespread disintegration of moral values bears a frightening resemblance to today's world. His writings constantly warn decent men that the corridors of commerce are filled with traitors and tricksters.

As in Gracián's time, today people in positions of power can be toppled by the whim of someone of higher rank. Gracián warns that we must recognize the shadows that precede these events. Business opportunities are often lost when we are outmaneuvered by clever adversaries. Anticipation is the key to circumventing backstabbing and other personal catastrophes. In a world of conflict and crisis, honed principles of survival are compulsory for successful interaction with one another. In the end, we must win.

Almost three decades have passed since I was introduced to the worthy ideas and beliefs of this seventeenth-century Jesuit. A book, "A Truthtelling Manual and the Art of Worldly Wisdom," edited in 1934 by Martin Fischer, came into my hands, a gift from a kindred soul who believed that as a professional lyricist I would enjoy these finely tuned writings. (Or perhaps that I might borrow from this man's wisdom for my own life and career.) Whatever the reason, I am glad of this opportunity to express my gratitude for this gift.

Years of adopting *Gracián's Manual* as my bible, and later studying the translation of the 1653 Spanish original,* found me restating this intriguing "guide for conduct" to all who would listen. I marveled at its author's transcendental ability to boldly shape an attitude, to

*Oraculo Manual y Arte de Prudencia.

score a situation so skillfully, and to succinctly state a point. Gracián, indeed, had touched me.

Following Gracián's line of thought, spiritual preparedness, and calm alertness lead to business, political, and personal power. For men and women who are maneuvering to safeguard their positions in the business world, and for others who are trying to establish them, these cerebral tools can be effective only as long as the undertow of rivalry and shrewd opposition is recognized.

In order to make Gracián's profound ideas understandable, I adapted his material, but never strayed from his beliefs. To introduce the aphorisms (small sermons) by subject, each chapter begins with an entry of "Gracián's recollections," an account I have created from my research into his history and an interpretation of his writings. In order to give credence to some historical facts, I have had to assume certain incidents, relationships, and places in Gracián's life experience.

The first entry begins at the end of his tumultuous life, a few months before his death in late December 1658.

Throughout, Gracián is a fascinating role model for survival. His own heroic story becomes the framework for his teachings, drawing readers into his surgical probings of life, with insights that are as applicable in today's world as they were centuries ago.

The astute reader will occasionally find contradictions in Gracián's words and wisdom. Gracián explains that contradictions stem from our ability to change. No two situations are alike, and points of view change at different moments.

The man had guts, and he believed in himself. He zealously believed in God. He believed that mankind could prosper with education and enlightenment. A few historians have said that the condition of being silenced at the hands of the church leaders was the springboard for the harsh tone of his controversial yet frequently correct judgments of man. Each reader will judge this for him- or herself.

As I moved deeper into my study of Gracián, I have come to fix my attitudes toward social and business situations in a way that allows me to move *through* each day with greater clarity. I have become, as Gracián advocates, master of my fate, making decisions freely, exploring options and choices, *in control* of what is happening to me at any given moment. I have learned to listen to an inner voice and to act upon what I know as the truth.

It is my hope that you, the readers of this book, will have a similar experience—that these small sermons of common sense decisions will become a source of light to guide you through the blind alleys of business and life.

In meeting the enlightened Baltasar Gracián you may also feel the inspiration and gain the spiritual strength to walk up to a "stone wall, paint a door on it, and walk through."

J. LEONARD KAYE
Rancho Mirage, California

THE
WISDOM
OF
Baltasar
Gracián

◆

A PRACTICAL MANUAL
FOR GOOD
AND PERILOUS TIMES

GRACIÁN'S RECOLLECTIONS

THE FIRST ENTRY:

✦

the final chapter of my life

On this twenty-fifth day of August, 1658, in the late evening of my life and at the age of fifty-seven, I, Baltasar Gracián, have a divine commitment to record the prime incidents that have taken me to this moment.

As I am about to prepare these entries of painful events in my life, I have no vision of who will read them. Yet I am

1

convinced that God will see to it that these recollections fall into the proper hands.

My health is failing. There is not much time remaining, perhaps a few months at best. Before I ascend to eternal peace, I am obliged, as all men are, to leave my contribution of earthly gratitude.

What better way to accomplish this than to warn future generations that the art of self-preservation is at the heart of survival? Or to point out that life is an ever-constant battle; and to alert those intent upon making their fortune in this world to the hidden intentions in human behavior. The world is an illusionary place and dangers abound.

I have devoted my life to the Church. The Church is good. But within its confines is a cold-hearted bishop who has vowed to destroy me. Archbishop Segovia Montoro has sought this revenge for years. Does he not know that God was watching him inflict misery on others?

I have dedicated my life to testimonies that needed to be heard by the populace, only to find, in the waning days, that nothing tangible remains: My voice has no listeners, my published writings are banned and have mysteriously vanished. The bishop decreed that those who did not turn in my books would be guilty of mortal sin. It is as though I never existed! But if this punishment was meant to break my will, it did not succeed.

I often think of the days gone by and the many events that shaped my life. I think of my constant conflict with certain leaders of the Church. Whoever said "He has the patience of a saint" must have had a survivor in mind, for how else does anyone prevail?

I have taken the priestly vows knowingly, and in my heart and mind have always followed the dictates of the Church. But I am obsessed, driven to speaking out against the chicanery in the world, and the imposters who deceive the good and seduce the trusting.

Should speaking out be judged a crime of ecumenical disobedience? In my thinking, it should not. But it is. And I am constantly on trial.

How can one not respond to his conscience? These are deep internal convictions, and I must listen to them. It is, after all, the voice of God.

My eyes are not blind and my heart is not stone; I observed my Jesuit brothers who bowed in obedience and bent their minds to the questionable interpretations they were directed to spout. I heard their raised voices warning the God-fearing parishioners of damnation: "Choose your own path," they shouted, "and you incur the wrath of the devil." Over and over they advocated: "Listen to what the Church instructs! God has chosen Mother Church to point out what is right thinking and that which is not!"

As I listened with heavy heart, I could not stand in the shadows and be crushed by the unbearable weight of my unspoken thoughts. If there is truth to the message of my brothers, why has God given us minds of our own?

My quest has always been to seek truth and to educate those who are eager to learn. I am convinced now that this quest is not something I chose for myself.

Some of my brother Jesuits would have the whole world become Christian by having Christians become worldly. If there were any certainty that it could be so, I would be in total agreement. But those who make promises they cannot deliver are mere hypocrites. The reality is that education is reserved for the rich, and celibacy denies mankind the offspring from some of our brightest minds.

The Bishop's hostility toward me is a mystery. Strangely, I have seen His Excellency but once in my life, but his messages and couriers have appeared at my door frequently; he is aware of my every movement.

I often wondered what so inflames the Bishop's heart. Is it mere pettiness? Is it jealousy? If he truly believes that I have effectuated harm toward the Church, it is purely imagined. I am a trained Jesuit, a teacher. I am here to enrich the soul of every reachable human being.

To you who read this journal I will explain my downfall and disgrace at the hands of the Bishop so that you can judge the events for yourself.

His fury was precipitated by a three-volume novel I had written, The Criticizer, *an allegorical vision of human life. My message affirmed that in a wondrous world, often darkened with corruption and evil, one should still have optimistic confidence in man's possibilities when he is aided by intelligence and kindness.*

And how did Archibishop Segovia Montoro respond to these principles? He threatened to report me to the General of the Society and to charge me with heresy. To avoid this unpardonable sin I complied with his demands that I go on a bread-and-water fast. Not once, but four full days.

The solitude, the humiliation, were awesome. I asked God's forbearance and I accepted my miserable punish-

ment with the knowledge that successful missions do not come without painful opposition.

But the Bishop was not finished with me. With stored vengeance he directed that I be removed from my faculty position at the University in Zaragoza. And when my written appeals finally exasperated him, he exiled me to a forgotten parish in Graus, a poor village in a deplorable state, millennia from any semblance of culture or vitality.

For my convictions, for my writings and my warnings to those who came to hear the Truth, I was stripped of my published works, and not even allowed a single copy of all that I had written.

Dear God, perhaps I do not belong in the Church. Perhaps my devotion somehow is incomplete. What a myriad of problems you give me!

Frightened, and in desperation, I applied to another order.

The Bishop's final revenge was to see that no other religious community accepted me. Neither did my friends in high places, not even King Philip IV, whom I knew quite well, come to my defense. I learned that friends do not come to the aid of a drowning man for fear that they themselves be caught in the undertow. But oftimes strangers do.

I must thank God for Señor and Señora Blanca, those elderly parishioners who remembered me from days gone by.

It is only a fortnight since they miraculously found me in an insignificant monastery performing menial chores in that forsaken village of Graus. They opened their hearts and home to me with unconditional kindness. My room in their *weather-worn house here in Tarragona is small and barren, yet I feel boundless gratitude for their warmth and friendship.*

In reflection, the Bishop always tried to stop me from writing. This drove me to do my work in the darkest hours of the night, by candlelight. The dim light and candle smoke burned my eyes, and the late hours left me fatigued.

Although it was the publication of The Criticizer *that caused the upheaval in my life, it is the disappearance of* The Oracle *that I mourn the most. In it was recorded all that I have observed in my lifetime: the good and the evil, the elegant and the vulgar. I cannot bear to think that copies of this work will lie buried forever in some dark, damp cellar, or worse, that they have become a pile of ashes.*

Yet strong resolve remains. Someday, somewhere, somehow . . . I am convinced that my voice will be heard through the words I have written.

Words, once recorded, are never lost from the human mind. This quiet room, this quill and parchment, will assist me. I know God will not take me until I have set down, once more, the "rules of life" from The Oracle.

Job was right: Life is warfare. But for the true survivor the worst that can happen is merely another obstacle that must be hurdled.

I feel the strength to create again, and I thank God for hearing my prayers.

The lost words easily come to mind. . . .

THE ORACLE

Gracián On:

SURVIVAL

SLEEP IS A SILENT PARTNER

When the problems of the day disturb the night, it is well to remember that the pillow is a silent partner. To sleep *on* an idea is worth more than to be sleepless under it.

THE SHORTEST ROAD TO BEING 'SOMEBODY' IS KNOWING WHO TO FOLLOW

Contact with the affluent is the most effective way in which to learn manners and taste. One takes on the thought and even the spirit of others without being aware of it. Let the one who is excessive join with the conservative, the impulsive with the restrained, the intemperate with the rational. Contrasts make the world beautiful, and if they can bring about such harmony in the physical world, they will accomplish even greater harmony in the moral. Avail yourself of such contrasts in the choice of your friends and associates, so that through the meeting of the extremes there may arise a meaningful path of untold possibilities.

FOR THOSE WHO ARE FOREWARNED THERE ARE NO DANGERS

All life should be continuous thinking in order to light upon the right way. It is reflection and foresight that assure success and freedom. Yet few think ahead. The wisest of precautions is to anticipate, with matured consideration, the worst that destiny can deliver. For those who are ready, there are no accidents; and for those who are forewarned, there are no dangers. Some act first and think afterward, which means that they must concern themselves more with the excuses for their acts than with the consequences that follow.

OUTWITTED IS OUTDONE

Watch him who conducts business in an indirect manner. The obvious is never present as he attempts to put you off guard so that he may steal from you. Such a man conceals his intent only to attain it. His intent lurks in the background in order to emerge casually when the moment is propitious: it becomes a shot that reaches its mark through its very carelessness. You are warned not to be asleep when the other's intent is so awake! Note with caution the craftiness, and recognize the pretexts that are advanced for this purpose. Consider the circumstances and know what you are conceding: take account of the source and qualify what you are granting. And in this mode allow him to understand that you understand. For he who is outwitted is outdone.

NO MAN IS WISE AT ALL HOURS

There are days when everything goes right for some, and with little effort, and when everything goes wrong for others. For those whose star is in the ascendant the spirit is well disposed, the mind is alert, and all they touch turns to gold. This is the hour to strike, and not to squander the least advantage. But each man must recognize his unlucky days, for even the strongest mind has its periods of uncertainty. No man is wise at all hours, since, at times, it takes luck even to think straight. On days when nothing goes right, even though the game may change, the bad luck may not. It is a time not to throw the dice, not to press for decisions. It is a time to retreat and inwardly regroup, and to draw on the power of your internal compass for the alignment of the stars in your favor.

THE MAN WHO PUTS YOU IN HIS SHADOW GAINS THE GREATER RECOGNITION

Never join someone who eclipses you. Align yourself with one who increases your luster. The man who puts you in the shade, because he is either more virtuous or more vicious, gains the greater recognition. He plays the main role and you are relegated to support him. And if recognition is due you through your own efforts, it will appear to be through *his* merits. Standing in someone's shadow hides you from special notice or attention. Even in a subordinate position you must find an area where you shine.

CONCEDE TODAY, SUCCEED TOMORROW

*T*here is no better remedy for turmoil than to let it take its course and come to rest by itself, especially when public or private matters cause turbulence in the sea around you. In storms of passion it is wise to seek a safe harbor with smoother waters. Many times an evil is made worse by the remedies used; here, leave things to nature, or there, to God. The learned physician needs just as much wisdom in order *not* to prescribe as to prescribe, and often the greater art lies in doing nothing. The way to avoid an oncoming whirlwind is to step aside to safety, and let it blow itself out. To concede today may be the best way to succeed tomorrow. It takes little to muddy a spring of sweet water; it serves best being left alone.

SHARP WORDS MAKE MORE WOUNDS THAN SURGEONS CAN HEAL

With rivals, and as a matter of decency when with others, select your words with caution. Sharp words make more wounds than surgeons can heal. There is always time to add a word, but none in which to take one back. Speak, therefore, as in a testament, for the fewer the words, the fewer the consequences. Know that whatever words you speak you will also hear, for the wind does not blow only in one direction. There are those who do not spare opinions, for they cost nothing. So they think, until they are forced to swallow what has been levied by someone else. The astute in business use soft words and hard arguments, for neither a word nor a stone let go can be called back.

LIFE IS LESS FORBIDDING WITH SOMEONE AT YOUR SIDE

*T*here is gratification in sharing joyful events and an advantage to partnership. More important is to discover someone to help shoulder your misfortunes. The hour of danger, the shadow of distress, will seem less forbidding with someone at your side. Some wish to carry off all the applause, but end by carrying off all the sounds of disapproval instead. In such circumstances have a confidante or partner at hand to make excuses for you, or at least to aid you in bearing the humiliation, for neither fate nor the crowd readily attacks two! This explains why the intelligent physician, having missed the cure, does not miss calling another, who under the name of consultant helps him carry the coffin. Divide with another your burdens and your sorrows. For misfortune, always difficult, is doubly unbearable to him who stands alone.

Completion brings success: He who vacillates is lost

Some men consume all their energy in getting started and so never get anywhere. They plan but they do not build. Because nothing is followed through, everything is left to itself, even when their ideas are well conceived. Instead of finishing things, impatience of the spirit leaves them finished *by* things. Some men sweat to conquer a difficulty, only to rest content in their labors before the job is done. Knowing how to bring victory home proves that they can; but not doing so proves that they do not care. This is frivolousness. If the undertaking was good, why was it not completed? Or if bad, why was it begun? The man who vacillates does not achieve success; he forgets that it is only the earth that is moving while he is standing still.

There are beasts in the marketplace with whom one cannot live — nor live without

Accustom yourself to the character defects of those about you as you would accustom yourself to an ugly face you must gaze upon daily. This compromise makes life tolerable, especially if your role in business is that of a subordinate. For there are beasts in the marketplace with whom one cannot live, nor live without. It is, therefore, the part of wisdom to accept them in order that you restrain yourself when pushed to the edge of confrontation. When the ugliness is first seen it terrifies, but little by little this fear grows less. In time you harden yourself against the unpleasantness, and the sight of the beast is no more threatening than its painted image on canvas.

KEEP YOUR WOUNDS TO YOURSELF

never will the cautious man in business reveal his feelings or disclose his ills, be they acquired or inherited. Fate itself is pleased at times to punish us where it pains most. No use to be angered by the insensitivity of colleagues, for this will only add to the general amusement. Evil intent in men is compelled to uncover the weakness of the competitor and discover where the suffering is greatest, in endless ways, until it hits the spot. The wise man never discloses what worries him or refreshes him, the former that it may pass, the latter that it may last.

ARRIVE WANTED, IN ORDER TO ARRIVE WELCOME

To appear at a function without being invited is as rude as to leave in the midst of it. Be unobtrusive so as not to be snubbed. The man who pushes himself in with boldness inspires others to find devious means of pushing him out in confusion.

KNOWLEDGE MUST ENCOMPASS THE MUNDANE AS WELL AS THE SUBLIME

Poets, dreamers, and scholars occupied in philosophy are easy to cheat. For even though they divinely discourse upon the unusual, they are often ignorant of the usual matters of life, which is much more necessary. The contemplation of things sublime leaves them no time for thought of mundane affairs. If you ascribe to this elite group, you need to develop a touch of the ordinary and commercial, just enough to keep from being cheated, or even from being laughed at as you make the daily rounds of life. Although there may be more to aspire to in this world, preciseness and good sense at all levels are necessary. Of what use is knowledge unless it be made to function? In truth, to know how to function in today's world is the truest of sciences.

APPROACH THE EASY AS THOUGH IT WERE DIFFICULT, AND THE DIFFICULT AS THOUGH IT WERE EASY

The easy task is often bungled by carelessness and overconfidence, the difficult by weakness and fear. Nothing more is required in order to do something poorly than to carelessly think it done; to thoughtfully go at the job, on the other hand, may accomplish the impossible. Undertakings should be carefully considered, but not be overly pondered; doing so creates apprehension and fear. Contemplating difficulties will produce them. Fear is the great suppressor of success, for it prevents you from realistically visualizing yourself in a leading position.

NEVER AWAKEN MISFORTUNE WHEN SHE SLEEPS

Do not take lightly the smallest problem that crosses your path, for it never comes singly, but in battalions. Essentially, concentrate on the core of good luck and bad, as understanding of both is necessary. It is the rule that all men flee the unfortunate and tie up with the fortunate, for everything fails the unlucky: himself, his reason, and his guiding star. It is prudent never to awaken misfortune when she sleeps. A slip is of little consequence, but to have this followed by a fall is fatal, for you do not know how far that will carry you. At times, just as nothing that is good seems ever to come to fulfillment, so nothing that is bad seems ever to come to an end. That which seems to come to us from Heaven requires reverence, while that which springs from earth requires intelligence.

DEAL ONLY WITH THOSE WHO HAVE AS MUCH TO GAIN OR LOSE AS YOU DO

never trust your honor to another without a clear passageway to his. Proceed so that the advantage of silence, or the danger of breaking it, is mutual. For this reason it is well to deal with men who have as much to gain or lose as you do. To collaborate with a person out of your class is to bring silent envy and unspoken antagonism into your life. The unsuccessful, as hard as they pretend, are never comfortable with the man who has proven himself to the world. Play in your own arena whenever you can. Never trust your honor to another, but if at some time you should do so, let it be with the insight demanded when intelligence makes concession to caution. Let the risk be mutual. Let the need be reciprocal, so that he who becomes your accomplice will not convert himself into a witness against you.

STUDY THE MOVEMENTS OF THE EYES TO DECIPHER THE SOUL THAT THEY MIRROR

Interpret the spirit and intent of those with whom you deal. If their cause is understood, the effect will be known; if a motive exists, it will surface. Concentrate on the countenance. Study the movements of the eyes, decipher the soul that they mirror. Read the furrowed brow, the mouth formations, the tone and pace of speaking; each is an imprint of the whole picture. Being fair of face does not negate a man's ability to be cunning. Hold him who laughs ceaselessly a fool, and him who never laughs as a devious man on guard against even well-meant and genuine inquiry. Expect little good of the misshapen soul, for these men are given to tossing harm in the way of almost all who cross their path. Know, too, that the man of practiced sincerity always speaks of matters in a manner far different from what they are. He uses terms of passion and not those of reason; thus he babbles according to his feelings, or his mood, and all very far from the truth.

GRACIÁN'S RECOLLECTIONS

THE SECOND ENTRY:

✦

my early years

Jf I feel strong today I can thank Señora Blanca. It is the soup. Filled with fresh vegetables from the garden, it sticks to the ribs and seems made to be served with her fine fresh-baked bread.

This morning a scruffy young man knocked at the front door demanding money to aid his lame sister. Señor Blanca happened to know the family, and this ruffian has no sister. Upon Señor Blanca's refusal of money, the young man shoved him to the floor and berated him foully. What is happening to our young people these days?

I see a deterioration of values that worsens with every passing year. There is a restlessness in the youth of our *nation that manifests itself in mindless crimes against innocent people. Perhaps the turmoil of the country portends a shortened life for youth, and this leads to uncivilized behavior. It does not speak well for the future.*

When I was a boy I prided myself on my personal behavior. I did not act in excitement, and I knew the value of courtesy. My father merely had to look at me a certain way and I would immediately correct any path that led to insolence.

The Graciáns of Belmonte were a respected family. My father, who was a doctor, not only repaired broken bones but also cured errant souls. I sometimes accompanied him on calls and was witness to the lectures that he delivered to his patients—lectures in honesty, goodness, integrity, and whatever virtues came to his mind at that moment. He was known as the man with God's golden hands and God's sweet voice.

My mother blended into the tranquillity of our modest home. I remember that she always wore black clothing, and that she prayed often. I could not tell whether she was quietly contented or quietly unhappy. It was my father who set the tone in our house.

I was the youngest of five children, the smallest, and like my mother, the quietest. My three brothers and I attended the local Jesuit school; my sister, the local convent for girls. After long hours of study, they found pleasure in the company of their outside friends. I found my friends in the worn copies of Seneca and Aristotle, and, of course, the Bible.

Books were not readily available in Belmonte, but a doctor never came home empty-handed for his services. Some-

times my father would return with chickens, rabbits, woven cloth, and sometimes with books from the wealthy land-owners.

I especially remember an inscribed Spanish edition of a play by an English playwright, William Shakespeare. The story of the Danish prince, Hamlet, was so engrossing that I reread it for days and nights at a time. Its powerful expression, its mysterious phrases intrigued and inspired me beyond description. I asked God to infuse my heart and mind with the ability to create such beautiful language. I prayed I would someday speak with grace and elegance to all who would listen. The year was 1618, and I was seventeen years old.

I remember my seventeenth year of birth for another reason. Spain was once again in financial crisis, and King Philip III did not believe in paying healthy young soldiers for merely patrolling the streets of Madrid and Barcelona while "eyeing the young girls," to quote my father. So off they were sent to the Indies in search of new land for the crown, or across the border into Europe. They went as conquerors to be housed and fed by the enemy and later to return with booty for the King's ornate palace.

During this period I noticed that my three brothers and sister were being made to spend much more time at home after school. I soon learned the reason. Their friends were joining the military. It was the way of life for adventurous young people in the year 1618.

My father, always aware of the dangers of social unrest and not wanting to see his children in the military, gathered us together one night, and after a prolonged dinner, an-

nounced his plans for us. Pedro and Felipe, who were very close, would enter the monastery in Cádiz. Raimundo, the handsome one, would go to Catalonia. Magdalena would enter the convent in Córdoba, and I, being the youngest, would join my uncle Antonio, a respected chaplain in the chapel of San Pedro de los Reyes in Toledo.

My mother listened in silence. There was deep sadness in her dark eyes. What my father could not know that evening was that none of us would ever see each other again.

Upon arriving in Toledo, I was thrust into a schedule of learning that took up every waking moment. My uncle Antonio had independently decided to have me become the outstanding student of the church's school. Although I was still in my youth, my prime studies were of humanities and philosophy. I understood his family-inspired motives and obediently submitted myself to his desire for my education.

Unbeknownst to me, discipline and study were forming a base that would harden me to the adversities the world has in store for all men.

In the year 1619, entering the novitiate of the Jesuits in Tarragona at the age of eighteen, I accepted the vows of poverty and self-sacrifice, of strict obedience to my superiors, and of celibacy. These I totally embraced. I was prepared for my study period, which would last from ten to twelve years, and the harsh realization that only one superior's determination could qualify me for the rank of professed.

In the course of the year with the Jesuits in Tarragona, my own independent behavior did not speak well for me, certainly not in the eyes of some of my superiors in the

Church. I had been taught gentlemanly manners and behavior, yet I was considered a failure in this area, according to Monsignor Palencia.

The Monsignor flatly stated that I could not conform. His written portrait of me painted a damaging picture that followed me throughout my career. "Baltasar Gracián is temperamental," he wrote. "Strong and sanguinary, with a certain melancholic passion."

The sanctimonious monsignor knew little about me. Why did he not ask to speak with my father? My father, in his deep voice, would have said politely: "Yes, my son, Baltasar does not conform easily," but my wise father would have added firmly, "especially if he does not believe."

These events led me to my own determinations:

I determined to excel in personal behavior.
I determined to reveal little of myself.
I determined to keep my head when fools lost theirs.
I determined never to vary from my principles.
I determined to accept responsibility for my actions.
I determined to achieve excellence in my post.
I determined to avoid excess of what is most pleasing.
I determined to do nothing in passion.
I determined to train my memory, never forget a name.
I determined not to cheat others and not to be cheated.
I determined that evil would never be my pleasure.
I determined to avoid extreme stubbornness.
I determined to let my cunning lie in not being cunning.
I determined to be a friend to myself.

During this period I observed often that leaders of the Church were so obsessed with the afterlife that they virtually ignored the pressing realities of the day. I came face to face with the evils of wealth and its influence on Church affairs. I observed, with shock, the internal battles for power and position in the Church itself. And then there were the working classes who were caught in the turbulence of warring nations, who were expected to give all they had—their worldly possessions and their lives.

Later, when I had attained a platform to denounce the ills of the world, I was prepared.

I remember well the warnings to my congregation. . . .

THE ORACLE

Gracián On:

PERSONAL BEHAVIOR

THE REAL DANGER OF A WORLD IN CHAOS IS THE UNHINGING OF YOUR OWN INTEGRITY

*T*he world is in chaos. Honorable dealing is deteriorating, good friends are few, truth is held in disrepute, good service is underpaid, poor service is overpaid. Whole nations are committed to evil dealings: With one you fear insecurity, with another, inconsistency, with a third, betrayal. This being what it is, let the bad faith of others serve not as an example, but as warning. The real danger of the situation lies in the unhinging of your own integrity: accepting less than your best, being overly tolerant of stupidity, forgiving incompetence, fraternizing with the nonspiritual. The man of principle never forgets what he is, because he clearly sees what the others are.

WHEN A FALSEHOOD IS EXPOSED, ACCEPT IMMEDIATE RESPONSIBILITY

Jt is said that a lie stands on one leg, truth on two; and he who says nothing never lies. In order to repair one foolish step, four more are taken, thus expanding the situation. One excuse made for another is sheer folly, for the accumulation quickly turns into a house of cards: each excuse needs the support of many in order for the house to stand. Worse than the defense of a falsehood is its protection. The repetitive denial of a lie tends to sink the culprit into a mire of hyperbole. And even if he is believed, the seed has been sown. One such vice will produce many in interest. When directly challenged or exposed by carelessness of the tongue, accept immediate responsibility. An explanation of motives offers more character than denial. The wise man may slip once, but not twice.

THOSE WHO RESORT TO EXTREMES PICK UP FOOLS AS ADMIRERS

There are times when ordinary men go to extremes in order to avoid the role of ordinary. Their effort becomes flippant and obvious. Whether in the clothes they wear or the behavior they manifest, they become laughable to those who observe this need to be unique. Every act that deviates from the serious borders upon the foolish. This especially holds true in business circles where product is the focus, and personal distraction harmful. At first the unusual is admired because of its freshness, but later, when the motive underneath it is realized, it is scorned. Those who cannot do something great in their drive for success resort to the paradoxical. They also pick up fools as admirers.

STUBBORNNESS IS A SELF-INFLICTED WOUND

*T*here are those who have clothed themselves in obstinacy so great that their minds cannot be penetrated even by the glaring light of simple reason. Every obstinacy is a boil, and those who are so marked often are blind to this blemish in their character. There are those who reduce everything to *war,* and they do not know the way of peaceful pursuit. They make foes of those who should be made their friends, and arrange their ends by intrigue and craftiness. But one day the tide rises against them, it thwarts their plans, and so they accomplish nothing. They become overladen with trouble, and everyone adds to their burden. These men have warped minds and accursed hearts. Avoid their savagery.

AVOID BEING THE SUBJECT OF YOUR CONVERSATION

If you talk about yourself you either praise, which is vanity, or you discredit, which is foolhardy. In both instances you reveal too much of yourself, which brings discomfort, and can even give pain to the listener. Talking about yourself is to be avoided in private life; and it is to be shunned even more in public office. When you speak to the crowd you risk seeming the fool if you even touch on this poor choice of subject matter. A similar weakness lies in speaking about those present; there is the danger of foundering on either of two rocks, that of silly overappreciation or that of unintentioned depreciation. Respect the danger. It is said that a fool who falls into the fire rarely falls out of it.

DO NOT ACT IN THE HEAT OF PASSION

*T*he heart and the head are often at odds; do nothing in passion or everything goes wrong. He cannot work for himself who is not in command of himself, and passion invariably overrides reason. When embarking on something of importance, collaborate with one who is hardheaded and less impassioned. They who judge from a distance always see more, as does the audience viewing a play, for those in the play are ruled by excitement. As quickly as you discover your temper beginning to stir, engage in hasty retreat, for the blood has rushed into your head and emotion has replaced the ability to think logically and clearly. A lifetime of damage can begin in one brief moment.

EMINENCE IS BUILT ON EXCELLENCE

Coldness from outsiders is often the rule toward those who succeed, for the peg that sticks out of the wood is the one hammered down. The world is filled with envy, and attaining favor in the eyes of men is always difficult. But there are ways of gaining this prize of respect and goodwill: excellence in a job, excellence in talent, and charm of manner assure it. Eminence is built upon such properties. It is soon discovered that the man needed the office less than the office needed the man. The job brings honor to some men, and other men bring honor to their jobs.

IF HE WHO FOLLOWS IN YOUR POSITION IS BAD, IT DOES NOT PROVE THAT YOU WERE GOOD

There is no glory in being considered good at your work just because he who followed in your position is bad. This does not prove that you are wanted back, but only that the other man is wanted out.

LET COLD DELIBERATION TAKE THE PLACE OF HEATED OUTBURST

Know how and when to stop anger as it rises in passion. At its height, one careless word turns its fire into an inferno. Prepare for the time when confrontation produces more heat than light. The first step is to announce that you are incensed, for it is then that conscious control enters the situation. Whenever possible, let cold deliberation take the place of heated outburst. Proof of maturity is to keep your head when the fools have lost theirs, for every flare of temper is a step downward from the rational. With considered judgment, your wrath will not go beyond reason. To be master of angry moods, yours or theirs, it is necessary always to hold tight the reins of disagreement so that it does not run wild.

HE WHO SPEAKS EVIL ABOUT ANOTHER ATTRACTS EVIL TO HIMSELF

The man who acts as a scandal sheet mostly destroys his own reputation. All take vengeance upon the slanderer by speaking ill of him. And since he stands alone, and they are many, he is conquered more quickly than they who are convinced of his defamations. The slanderer walks in the aura of mistrust; and even at times when important men are seen in his company, it is assumed that it is more because his constant mockery amuses them than because his wisdom enchants them. Evil should never be our pleasure, nor our theme. Whether it be by innuendo, whispering campaign, or uncomplimentary remark, he who speaks evil about another attracts evil to himself.

RECOGNIZE THE POWER OF COURTESY

Courtesy is the quiet, underlying power behind all negotiations. Those of breeding fall under its spell, while the vulgar, confronted by it, fall over in confusion. It is said that only a fool keeps shouting while his opponent whispers. When you add courtesy to something you sell, it returns a twofold value. You receive the worth of the goods and, at the same time, the respect of the satisfied buyer. Among mature negotiators, courtesy is a sign of sophistication and caring. Even in an exchange in which few words are spoken, the buyer and seller agree tacitly to trade again. There isn't much that the art of courtesy cannot improve.

AT TIMES, THE REMEDY FOR AN EVIL IS TO FORGET IT

Memory plays the villain by forsaking us when we need her most. One must also know how to forget, though it is more a matter of luck than it is skill or art. In all that gives pain, memory is most lavish, and in all that gives joy, it is miserly. At times the remedy for an evil is forgetting it, but the state of forgetfulness does not easily appear. The cerebral door is wide open in times of adversity. It is as though the mind, weakened by grief, is fair game for any other misery that wishes to attach itself to us. Train your memory, difficult as it may be, for it has the power to bring you heaven or hell.

THERE IS NO GLORY IN CHEATING AN HONEST MAN

In the hearts of others do not be held a cheat, even though it is difficult to live today without being deceptive at times. It is far better to be prudent than crafty. It is better to be esteemed for your wisdom than feared for your treachery, for reputations fly on invisible wings and find their way to unexpected places. Let your greatest cunning lie in not being cunning. There is nothing easier than deceiving an honest man. He who never lies believes everything, and he who never deceives trusts everyone. Be known as a man who inspires trust, rather than one of hollow pretense who feigns truth.

A HOUSE GUEST EARNS HIS INVITATIONS BY WIT, WISDOM, AND HIS LISTENING ABILITY

In the marketplace demand is the yardstick of value. Lack of demand diminishes the worth of the most precious thing. So it is as a guest in another man's house. A house guest earns his invitations by the naturalness of his wit and wisdom, and, failing these, by his listening ability. He succeeds not because he is the brightest, but because his presence suggests comfort to his patron. He is a calm sea that does not create waves. In another man's house it is sensible to satisfy the hunger of the body, but not to satiate it. Partaking in excess of what is most pleasing suggests gluttony. The way to please your host is to leave with an appetite still retained for his offerings as well as his company.

FOLLOW YOUR OWN BENT, NO MATTER WHAT PEOPLE SAY

If you believe in your daydream, follow your own bent no matter what people say. He who is self-reliant, when carrying himself, carries everything with him. Be such a friend to yourself, and you will be able to solve problems large and small. You will need to be beholden to no one when your own mind and your own judgment have learned the bends of the road that protect you from harm's way.

HANDSHAKES ARE NOT CONTRACTS

make yourself wise in the matters of the world. Learn that approval is not a promise, and handshakes are not contracts. Learn that there are hidden agendas in the human mind.

ILL MANNERS CAUSE DISFAVOR

Ill manners cause disfavor, a great price to pay for uncontrolled behavior. Do not provoke disapproval. Even without invitation it will come quickly enough, for there are many who hate without reason, even when one tries hard to please.

The urge to injure others is often more powerful than the desire to gain our own advantage

*T*oday, the urge to injure one another seems more powerful and swifter than the desire to gain advantage for ourselves. Some are happy only when they are at odds with the world. They find strange excitement and, more often than not, relief from boredom in stirring up trouble. There are varied ways men are judged: men of clear judgment are feared, the evil-tongued are loathed, the presumptuous are shunned, the buffoons are detested, and the singular are left to themselves.

SEEK A QUIET LIFE

Try to live in harmony with the elements. Show appreciation in order to be appreciated. If you desire affection, show affection. Anything for a quiet life!

VIRTUE, NOT FORTUNE, MAKES A MAN WORTH LOVING

Moral excellence, righteousness, goodness: these are the sweet sounds of virtue. She is the bond of all perfections and the heart of all life's satisfactions. Virtue makes men sensible, alert, understanding, wise, courageous, considerate, joyous, truthful, and visionary. Virtue is the sun of our lesser world, the sky of good conscience. She is so beautiful that she finds favor with both God and man. There is nothing lovely without her, for she is the essence of wisdom, and all else is folly. Greatness must be measured in terms of virtue, and not in terms of fortune. Virtue alone makes a man worth loving in life, and worth remembering after death.

GRACIÁN'S RECOLLECTIONS

THE THIRD ENTRY:

◆

MY DAYS AS A NOVICE

This morning, as I was about to sit at my table, a little yellow-speckled bird flew through the open window into my room, looked about, and hurriedly returned to the open skies. It was a sweet moment.

During the night I was awakened by a disturbing dream about my handsome older brother, Raimundo. In my dream he was enamored of a simple, round-faced peasant girl who attended his church just so that she could gaze at him as he stood on the pulpit. They ran off together. It was not at all a way of life that I had envisioned for him. I called to him but he did not hear me.

I do not study dreams, but I realize that this dream of escape is not an uncommon occurrence in wakeful life. In fact, in my younger days as a novice, thoughts of fleeing occasionally crossed my mind, especially when the incessant teachings by my superiors bore down like hammers on my head. Had it not been for a small incident I might have done something rash to escape the continuous mental strain thrust upon me.

During my studies with the Jesuits in Tarragona the unfortunate death of Brother Bartolome Vallsebre of the Society turned into an opportunity for me. The respected priest died of a mysterious illness and I was requested to write his eulogy. This was my first writing assignment.

I had two days in which to complete it. My memorial for Brother Vallsebre would be read before the congregation.

On the appointed day, the text, read feelingly by Bishop Garcia, was not the most eloquent, but it differed from a thousand traditional eulogies heard before. I had written: "The procession to the gate of heaven is constantly in progress, and one by one we take our place in line. . . . The Lord does not give a cross to those who cannot carry it. . . ." From the corner of my eye, with my head bowed, I observed rows of heads like tulip fields in the breeze nodding in tacit approval.

This was my first writing to receive public acknowledgment. I will always remember the date: April 21, 1620.

Although I continued to write, it was four years before my next public reading. Coincidentally, it was another memo-

rial, this one for Father de Alabiano, a popular priest who had lost his sight when he was a young man and subsequently, assisted by others, managed to memorize the complete Bible.

I still recall part of the necrology. "Father de Alabiano's world of darkness allowed him the divine privilege of holy vision of the splendor that is heaven. In the dark of his mind he witnessed the glory long before he was delivered. . . ."

The congregation wept. I am certain that it was not on account of my eulogy but for the loss of a popular priest and his remarkable memory. Still, I sensed my words had helped release the flood of grief all felt for this great man.

Between the debuts of my first public writings two important events occurred. My first vows were taken, and I transferred my studies to philosophy at the College of Calatayud in northern Spain.

I am suddenly reminded of my professor. I cannot recall his name but I remember well that I could anticipate almost everything that he said. He was a virtual encyclopedia of trite banalities. Sometimes, out of sheer boredom, I would voice his words in unison. This eventually prompted the professor to recommend my transfer to the University in Zaragoza. He wished me well, but his forced smile suggested that he was indeed happy to see me continue my theology studies elsewhere.

Although I had now been tutored by many professors, the Jesuit who still lingers in my mind is Father Pedro Sanz. I had met Father Sanz earlier in Toledo through the introduction of my uncle Antonio. His scholarly face belied his intensity.

Father Sanz normally spoke softly, but from the pulpit he virtually breathed fire. At first his delivery shocked me; he was unlike any preacher I had ever heard, and I was drawn to his every appearance in the pulpit, as was his audience. I recall his ability to modulate his voice from a mere whisper to the sound of roaring thunder. The effect was riveting.

Father Sanz's other remarkable ability was his way of combining clever wit with bitter lessons of experience. I was utterly transfixed. Years later that intense manner became the model for my preaching. Colleagues who knew Father Sanz often said that I went even further.

While serving as secretary to Father Blas de Vaylo, Vice-Rector in Zaragoza, my eyes were opened to the fact that not all Jesuits in the university practiced the ideals of Ignatius. For instance, the Vice-Rector might say anything just to settle a situation at the moment. His modus operandi was to keep things moving, to dismiss matters as quickly as possible.

In listening to him as he addressed laymen and church officials, and having myself become familiar with his beliefs, I was amazed to hear how casually the Vice-Rector would voice what to me seemed to be blatant lies. The shame of it was that this jolly-faced Jesuit was trusted and revered.

Untruths are painful to me, and this sensitivity in my nature ultimately led to a fatal error.

Believing that I might be helpful to the Vice-Rector, I tactfully questioned him about a conflicting set of orders he had given me to follow. Instantly his round face turned pur-

ple. How dare I? How dare I ridicule a superior? He had never thought much of me from the beginning. My insolence was intolerable! My dismissal as secretary was to be immediate! Then came a barrage of unbelievably foul words sputtered at me.

I stood there awestruck, my mouth open, my eyeglasses askew. My arms stretched toward him for mercy, but the verbal pounding continued. Had Father Santos not entered the office at that moment there is no telling how long the Vice-Rector would have continued berating me.

I agonized over the incident throughout the night. Only when I asked for and received forgiveness from God was I able to have some rest in the early hours of the morning.

My years of exhausting study, spiritual exercises, performing the most menial duties, and being ordered about like a soldier finally entitled me, in the year 1627, to attain the eminent goal of my life. At the age of twenty-six I was ordained a priest. My union with God was complete. I would serve Him well. But my work was just beginning.

There was still the probationary period preceding my public and apostolic life as a Jesuit. Verbal testaments and endless written examinations had to be taken before my final qualifications would be judged. And these would be judged by one superior: Father Blas de Vaylo, the Vice-Rector, whose memory I had foolishly attempted to aid.

I was well prepared for the reality of the precarious situation. In my every waking moment I was obsessed with preparing for the probationary period. When it came time for the series of examinations, I had no doubt whatsoever that

I would succeed with high honors. But the Vice-Rector gave me a failing mark.

The following year I again received a failing mark even though I was secretly told by a friendly priest that I had proven myself to be an exemplary student.

I succeeded in the third probationary period with the lowest score allowed as a passing mark. How humiliating! But I had finally become an apostolic Jesuit, bound by vows of poverty, chastity, and obedience.

Upon reflection, I feel that it is little wonder that I was driven to adopt a protective attitude for the unprotected. I secretly vowed, when the time came, that opposing deceit, tyranny, and trickery would be my way of life.

I would do, and leave talk to others.
I would deal solely with men of honor.
I would uphold moral excellence.
I would debate with reason and observation.
I would learn to be patient.
I would gain goodwill by serving.
I would learn to think clearly.
I would seek the good in everything.
I would carefully reconsider all decisions.
I would follow the path of the wise in order to become wiser.
I would add refinement to every situation.
I would let the conscience of goodness be my guide.
I would follow the rules of the Great Master.

As I sit here in this room, I am immensely comforted by how easily the writings of The Oracle come to mind. Surely God must have a hand in this. Surely this is His way of directing His fallen soldier to share these considerations with young warriors locked in the daily confrontations of survival.

I pray that the words I continue to record will inspire their chosen way of life, or the way of life that has been mysteriously chosen for them.

THE ORACLE

Gracián On:
a way of life

GENIUS DOES NOT TREAD IN THE FOOTSTEPS OF THE CROWD

There is a spark of genius in the great majority. But the talent for discovery is limited to individuals who choose *not* to tread in the footsteps of the crowd. And so it is that a man of inventive mind is marked with genius, and at the same time, even he will agree, a touch of insanity. It is not known how this creativity begins, and philosophers disagree on whether it is born in the soul of man or comes from the vastness of the universe. While normal mortals lie dormant somewhere in between, the genius has the capacity to stretch his creative thoughts and singular explorations to capture miracles.

HE WHO MUST WIN HAS NO RULES

*T*he man who must win at all costs has a boundless capacity for deception. He believes that the rules of integrity and propriety were written for others to obey. He believes that it is only by the strategic means of entering into the plans of another that he can come out with his own plans. Thus, he is familiar with the trick of gaining goodwill by serving. While it looks as though the other person's ends are being met, he is maneuvering to open the way for himself. He plays on dangerous ground, and often his strategies are bungled by a single false move in the presence of one who has been alerted.

TOO MUCH TIME IS SPENT ON THE PURSUIT OF WEALTH, TOO LITTLE ON THE THINKING SPIRIT

With limited exception, philosophy, built on a system of truths, stands discredited today, even though it was once the major pursuit of the sages. In today's generation there appears to be little time available beyond the pursuit of wealth and pleasure. Forgotten is the pleasure found in the art of thinking clearly or in deductive reasoning to gain knowledge. The tools of philosophy—reason, observation, faith, and intuition—lie rusted in sad ruins as the world speeds through the universe in search of itself. Although the science of thinking lives in loneliness, and at times is even degraded, it is to be noted that the question of how man acquires knowledge and learns truth is ever the food of the thinking spirit, and the joy of the high-minded and respectable.

HE LIVES LONG WHO LIVES WELL

nature, in her great wisdom, has bestowed upon man duplicates of many of those members of the body which are most important, and most exposed: eyes, ears, nostrils, arms, and legs. And following this design, one should not depend solely upon, or be limited to, any one thing, however extraordinary it may be. Possess yourself of the necessities of life twice over. It will ensure, doubly, your comfortable existence. Much should exist in duplication, especially the means of life, goodwill, and satisfaction. Accumulate a reserve of all that is meaningful, and let it be the policy of your life. He lives long who lives well.

DEVELOP SOMETHING ATTRACTIVE ABOUT YOURSELF

Develop something attractive about yourself, for it is the magic of civil interplay. Use this attraction more to catch goodwill than good things, but always use it. Sincerity rings truer when presented with charm. Efficiency supported by beauty suggests greater efficiency, and fares well for the opportunistic; for where the ground is already rich, fertilization aids most. By such means, acceptance and popular yearning are created until all hearts are won. However, know that there are countless substitutes for the rich and beautiful. Find your personal magnetism and develop it.

REJOICE IN WHAT YOU DO, BUT DO NOT BOAST OF IT

They who have done the least make the greatest to-do of what they have done! A quirk in their character venerates the simplest deed they perform, and everything is made to appear marvelous. Even when speaking of others, self-applause is apparent in the theme of the praises they sing. Conceit is always frowned upon, and those who crow like a rooster only succeed in aggravating the hearing of those whom they try to impress. Real achievement needs no such affectation. Rejoice in the fulfillment of what you do, and leave talk to others. Aspire to be heroic without calling for a heavenly choir to herald your accomplishments.

THE PATH OF THE WISE IS TO SEEK THE WISER

There is no greater frustration than to be heard and not understood, to have words of passion fall on deaf ears. More cherished is the thoughtful "yes" of one intelligent man than the shouts and applause of a whole arena. So we must look to the sages, the venerable men of sound judgment. We must seek and revere them if life is to have meaning. They hear more than one says, and they speak with understanding; their praise brings lifelong satisfaction. The path of the wise is to seek the wiser, otherwise why would Plato call Aristotle his whole school? Others, shallow and lacking insight, seek the ordinary and fear the intellectual; for such people it is easier to be less and to expect less in order to do less. Even rulers need the keen understanding of their biographers; for though they fear no man, they fear the biographer's pen more than ugly women fear a painter's brush.

GOOD FINDS GOOD

Search for the good in everything. There is nothing that does not hold some good if we but seek it. But the minds of some men are burdened with such unhappiness that, out of a thousand good points, they manage to strike upon a lone defect, and this they toss about like scavengers of men's minds and purposes. There is perverse joy for these collectors of refuse in compiling the sins of others so that they can feel superior. Avoid such grave diggers, for in time it is they who fall into the hollow opening. Be the man who, among a thousand evils, strikes upon the single good. Good finds good, but good that comes too late is as good as nothing.

IT IS A WEARYING BUSINESS TO GOVERN MEN

If you have a desire to officiate, know what the office holds. Opportunities are in abundance for the man who volunteers to give of himself, but nothing calls for greater care in choice. Some offices demand courage, and others shrewdness. It is easy to manage in those establishments which call merely for honesty, but most difficult in those which call for skill. It is a wearying business to govern men, who often include the neurotic and fool; and double brains are needed to deal with those who have none.

ONLY FOOLISH MEN ARE UPSET BY EVENTS THEY CANNOT CONTROL

He who grows in wisdom grows in impatience, just as he who knows much is hard to satisfy. At times we suffer most impatience with those upon whom we most depend. But this is a game of fools, for only foolish men are upset by events they cannot control. Learning to keep a rein on impatience when our nature is impetuous prepares us for encountering misfortunes with perfect calm. It is the lessons of restraint that force us to set up a school of self-control. Let him who cannot control his impatience take refuge within himself and test his strength in putting up with himself.

HE KNOWS WHO KNOWS THAT HE DOES NOT KNOW

It is only the fool who does not see that which others see. He dwells in a garden of roses oblivious to the thorns. Living in mystical reverie, he is like the frog in a well who sees the sky as a little patch of blue no larger than the roundness of his shelter. Small-minded and foreign to vision, he becomes the greatest fool because he does not see himself as one, while declaring all other such. For the wise man, it is not enough to appear wise. He must display characteristics that deliberately suggest there are things that he does not know. This act will gain approval from others and achieve for him large measures of respectability. His casual denial of complete wisdom will make him seem all the wiser in a world full of fools.

Applaud great men

Every decade produces a few great men who speak of freedom, love, and dignity for all, regardless of ancestry and religious beliefs. Applaud these great captains and perfect orators. In your recognition you will be lending your voice to theirs, and in minuscule degrees you will scrape away some of the ills that encrust the world. Many men have seized for themselves the likeness of heroes, but their actions will prove to be in vain. For without great deeds for the greatest number, their voice is no more than a wisp of air.

TO CAVORT WITH THE VULGAR IS TO INFECT BOTH DIGNITY AND REPUTATION

We are surrounded by the ordinary. It lies all about, even in the best of families. Ordinary as the ordinary may be, far worse is the vulgar, which combines the uncouth, the coarse, and the scurrilous. The vulgar man talks like a fool and insolently finds fault with almost everything. He is the great disciple of ignorance and the defender of untruths. We must quickly recognize the culprit and free ourselves from his presence. To cavort with the vulgar is to infect our dignity and reputation. It is far better to do without than to walk within the boundaries of the gross. The problem of the vulgar man is his and his alone. Pay no attention to what he says, and care less of what he thinks.

LEAVE SOMETHING TO BE DESIRED

Having everything you wish for leaves you empty of wishes. Leave something to be desired, for such passion stimulates the mind's curiosity and keeps hope alive. Let the climb to your ultimate goals be deliberate and measured so that your spirit continues to have its longings. Likewise, when rewarding someone for a kind deed, a special favor, it is wise not to gratify them totally. Appreciation should be delivered in small portions over a period of time so that it is remembered. When all is yours and desire ends, apprehension begins. When nothing more is to be wished for, everything is to be feared. This can be the most unfortunate of fortunes.

MATERIAL EXCESSIVENESS PRODUCES MORE SILENT ENEMIES THAN GENUINE FRIENDS

many of the extravagant things that bring delight should not be owned. They are enjoyed more if they belong to another rather than you. The first day they give pleasure to the owner, but in all the days that follow, to those around him. The rich man's possessions quickly blend into an array of other properties of value. And were it not for pointed praise from outsiders he would hardly be mindful of their existence. The material objects that belong to another are a double enjoyment for you because their luster is only seen on occasional visits; it retains freshness for you, while the same cannot be guaranteed to the owner. The possession of lavish things not only diminishes the enjoyment of them, but sometimes augments annoyance from others in the form of envy and vexation of spirit. Material excessiveness produces more silent enemies than genuine friends.

Reconsideration has its own reward

In business dealings, reconsideration provides a measure of safety by adding time and refinement to the situation. Where dissatisfaction is inevitable, it is prudent to deliberate either to soften judgment or to strengthen it. Time provides the opportunity to have new reasons emerge to support decisions. Reconsideration offers other rewards. If something is to be given, the gift that is considered beforehand will most likely be cherished more than the one chosen in the rush of the moment. If something offered by another must be refused, time provides the perfect opportunity for discovering how best to say no. Reconsideration given to him who pleads urgently and suspiciously may well turn into a stroke of luck; in time all tricks surface. There are not many things to which reconsideration cannot be applied to good advantage.

A FERTILE MIND, DEEP UNDERSTANDING, AND A CULTURED TASTE LEND FLAVOR TO ALL OF LIFE

*T*hree things make the superior man: a fertile mind, a deep understanding, and a cultured taste. There are minds that radiate light, like the eyes of the lynx, which in the greatest darkness see most clearly. Then there are those born for the occasion. Guided by uncanny understanding, they always strike upon what is most beneficial. And good taste lends flavor to all of life. A good imagination is another great advantage, but even greater is the ability to think clearly, for clear thinking is the sweet fruit of reason. We soon learn that we are ruled by our age. At twenty years desire rules us; at thirty, expediency; at forty, judgment; beyond, the experience of wisdom. The shoes of the superior man may not fit all, but all should make every attempt to walk in them.

GRACIÁN'S RECOLLECTIONS

THE FOURTH ENTRY:

◆

my professorship

This morning I read again some of the pages logged from my memory. I see the difference in my manner of writing these recollections and the way I have recalled the passages from The Oracle. *One is spontaneous, the other formal.*

This parallels life. All things have a double value. So it is that one person calls white the very same thing another calls black. It all depends on the point of view chosen.

This nagging truth has led me to many confrontations. I often think, if only I had held my tongue. . . .

I arrived at the Jesuit college in Lérida in 1631, completely dedicated to the greater glory of God—ad majorem Dei gloriam. I was thirty years old. My lean body and inquisitive mind were fit for any task that might arise.

I found myself standing before Father Sanchez, an elderly Jesuit in charge of admissions. He was in his office, seated behind a small wood desk scrutinizing my records, which had preceded my arrival.

"Your family name," he began, "does not have the sound of true Spanish heritage." He raised his eyes to analyze my reaction. "Yet you deny having Jewish or Moorish lineage . . ."

This was the basis of his probing inquiry and it seemed to have no conclusion. It was when I could tolerate it no longer that I stepped into that forbidden area between black and white. I challenged his knowledge of anthropology and tactfully inquired if he could, with certainty, ascertain his own ancestry.

He leaped from his chair and rushed out of the room. I recall his blabbering something to the effect that Father Superior must immediately hear of this insolence.

Upon reflection, I see that his reaction was true to the purpose and discipline of the Society of Jesus, which called for reporting the faults of associates to superiors, and for harboring no resentment for being reported.

In a few minutes the excitable Father Sanchez returned to the room followed by a stately priest whose refined features I immediately found friendly and likable. Father Superior stared at me for a moment, then simply asked: "Are you the new professor?" I nodded. "Follow me," he directed.

In his office he embraced me and welcomed me to the fold. "Do not pay too much attention to Father Sanchez," he explained. "He is a Jesuit priest, but he is not a very good one."

Father Superior and I were friends from that moment. He was not the usual solemn superior, and he even had a sense of humor.

I was later informed that the Father was a direct descendant of the famous Loyola family. It was Ignatius who, one hundred years or so earlier, had set out by foot from Venice to Rome with two other priests in order to seek audience with the Pope. This same Ignatius of Loyola achieved sainthood by founding my beloved Society of Jesus.

How quickly I had made an enemy and a friend. Father Sanchez never addressed me and remained a lifelong enemy. Father Superior chose me to be his adviser. But instead of discussing church matters we found ourselves enveloped in questions of philosophy, especially the omnipotent mystery of creation. We found instant agreement in the belief that we are all one, and that every living thing is alive because of every prior living thing.

Father Superior's companionship was joyous for my mind and uplifting for my soul. Though we met often, it should be noted that we were not derelict in our official duties. After a while we did discuss church matters, and we were of one mind.

Two years later, the good Father recommended me for

the elite position of professor of languages and philosophy at the University of Gandía. I taught French and Latin.

My tenure at the university was uneventful with one exception. In 1635 I received a surprise visit from the famous humanist, Don Vincencio Juan de Lastanosa. He quickly explained his visit by saying: "There are some interesting things being whispered about you, Father Gracián. I thought a personal meeting would be in order."

He was a Jesuit with a kind face, a generation apart in years, and interestingly, his church was in my beloved Aragon. That fact, and my immediate affinity to this fatherly figure, created a strong wish to follow this appealing man to his region. Only a teaching position could make this transfer possible.

My wish was heard, perhaps in the heart or mind of Father Lastanosa, because a fortnight later there was an opening for me at St. Luke's Jesuit College.

In Aragon, having Father Lastanosa as a mentor created unexpected rivalry. In vying for his attention some of the young priests ignored me while others often reported me to their superiors, complaining that I was spending too much time with the Father and not attending fully to my duties. This was not true. I also knew that rivalry was but a step away from enmity, and I therefore did all in my power to calm the situation.

With Father Lastanosa's permission I invited my contemporaries to join in our discussions, and I listened with body, eyes, and ears to what each of them had to say. But it was the extraordinary Father Lastanosa to whom I listened with my heart.

As a humanist, in contrast to those who viewed men as sinful creatures who ought to devote their lives to earning a place in heaven, he spoke warmly of man, of his nature and his place in the universe. Although he was critical he was also realistic. He was brilliant at recalling the clearest words of wisdom that had ever been spoken or written, and he quoted them with ease and elegance. No human being, before or since, has ever inspired me more.

While listening to him, I more clearly understood the nature of man, who is both good and evil and who must be dealt with accordingly if one is to survive. Each situation calls for its own solution. I vowed to rethink my own relationships with friends, rivals, and enemies.

I vowed to learn the art of debating.
I vowed always to have a trusted friend.
I vowed always to be open to suggestions.
I vowed to observe clearly before I firmly acted.
I vowed always to try to make a friend of a rival.
I vowed to listen to my enemies in order to hear my faults.
I vowed never to waste an important man's time.
I vowed to make parting a well-ordered retreat.
I vowed neither to love nor hate without end.

When one enjoys an extended life, the cupboard of relationships overflows with the memory of names and faces. These old friends became even more alive on the pages of the vanished Oracle. As I am about to revisit them and draw from their individuality, I clearly see them again. They were *good friends and they were good enemies. Each, guided or misguided, gave the best of himself; each followed his bent, and they all have a place in my heart.*

As Father Superior often remarked: We are all one.

THE ORACLE

Gracián On:

friends, rivals, and enemies

KEEPING FRIENDS IS MORE IMPORTANT THAN MAKING THEM

Some friends are good nearby, and some at a distance. For the latter, distance minimizes shortcomings. There are those, ill at ease in close conversation, who shine in correspondence. Such is the variety of friends, and the best variety undoubtedly are the well salted, even though their digestion costs you a measure of discomfort. However, keeping friends is more important than making them. Few know how to be good friends, and he who does not know how to choose friends is destined to make few friends. The art in keeping friends is to know how to call forth the best in them. This has its own good sense because it establishes the rules of exchange, as you, too, derive pleasure in having your best called forth. The friend who will last not only brings satisfaction but also stimulation. Search out those who promise to last even though at first they appear less mature. None lives so alone as he who lives without friends, for friendship multiplies the good and divides the bad.

Know how to conduct a successful interview

In seeking employment the man standing before you waiting to be interviewed is prepared for your interrogation. It is an undeclared battle of wits. Your alertness is matched by his reserve. The answers will not surface if the questions go unasked, for great judgment is required to take the measure of another. More important by far is to know the composition and the properties of men than to know those of minerals and vegetables. This is the most delicate of the occupations of life: for metals are known by their ring, and men by what they speak. Words reflect the mind of a man, and hint at the quality of his work. To know how to truly analyze a man calls for the clearest observation, the subtlest understanding, and the most critical judgment. The rewards are countless for the gifted who can analyze a man by dividing his complex whole into its parts or elements.

WITH MUCH AT STAKE, FEW PLAY FAIR

When there is much at stake, there are few who play fair. Warring opponents are often the same men who lived in honor and peace as long as they had no ambitious emulators; rivalry exposes the flaws which courtesy has covered over. Know that every effort you make to outshine your opponent does some damage to your own reputation, for the true purpose of competition is to find a way to belittle your opponent in order to weaken him. The heat of combat brings to life personal issues long dead and digs up stenches long gone. Even the dust of forgetfulness is shaken from old scandals. As the combat intensifies, competition brings forth a manifesto of slander and calls to its aid whatever it can, and not what it should. There is much to be considered before the sword is drawn. Men of peace should project for themselves the final scene of the play before they step onto the stage of battle.

THE ART OF DEBATE IS TO ENTANGLE THE OTHER

Know how to debate. It is the craft of exploration, intended not to entangle you but to entangle the other; it is a unique form of torture to make the opponent's feelings flinch. Sensitive probing of the mind's intent reveals the unexpected. Cautious questioning of oblique remarks ferrets out the most hidden secrets, driving them into the mouth of your rival until they fall from his tongue. Controlled reserve, on your part, can slowly entice the other to throw caution to the wind, exposing his feelings, even though by any other method his heart would have been closed. Pretending doubt, in order to discover what you seek or what you can learn, may surprisingly produce desired vulnerability.

EVERY FRIEND IS SOMETHING GOOD IN YOUR LIFE

Have friends, it is a second life. Every friend is something good. When much is shared, much is learned. For friends to continue to wish you well, show courtesy, respect, and understanding; the way must be found to their hearts. Try daily to make a friend—if not an intimate one, at least one who shows that he has your interest at heart. It is from a casual acquaintance that a trusting confidante emerges. Giving is still the safest side of friendship. It is said that true friends, generous in nature, tie their purse with a cobweb thread.

BEWARE OF UNDERLINGS WHO SEEK TO REPLACE YOU: HOLD CERTAIN THINGS IN RESERVE

When you reach the pinnacle of your industry or art, beware of underlings. Certain information should be withheld from those who may seek to replace you; learn to keep the ultimate refinements of your specialty to yourself. This is the law of the great masters, who must themselves retain the subtlety of their art even as they teach it. Feed the imagination of your subordinates, satisfy their anticipation, but just as art must be employed in the teaching of art, restraint must be exercised in the company of those who offer praise to gain access to that which makes an achievement yours alone. Only then can you maintain your reputation, and the dependence of others upon you. To hold certain things in reserve is a great law of life and of conquest.

NEITHER LOVE NOR HATE WITHOUT END

Confide in the uncertain friends of today as though they are the enemies of tomorrow. And because such things come to pass, be prepared. Do not provide the deserters of friendship with the ammunition by which to make better war. Yet neither love nor hate without end. Toward your enemies keep an open door of reconciliation, and let it be a wide one, for that is safest. Especially know that the thirst of yesterday's vengeance can become today's torment against you. Also know that time softens the enemy, and shines a new light on the old disagreement. And if the open door leads to trade resumed, you are now, at least, armed with caution.

THE MAN WHO WILL NOT LISTEN IS INCURABLY THE FOOL

*T*here are men who cannot be saved because they cannot be reached. They hurl themselves to destruction because none dares approach to restrain them. They leave no open door for even one friend to advise or point to the fault without difficulty and embarrassment. Be open to suggestion. Develop a trusted friend. No one is so perfect that he may not at times need a monitor. Keep within the closet of your soul the faithful mirror of someone to whom you may turn, and from whom you will take correction when in error, or guidance when faced with problems. He is incurably the fool who will not listen.

FEW ARE FRIENDS OF WHO YOU ARE: MOST ARE FRIENDS OF WHAT YOU ARE

There are friendships that are legitimate and others that are lightweight and matter little. The former enrich your accomplishments, the latter give only fleeting pleasure. In our world today, where ambition abounds, few are friends of who you are; most are friends of what you have accomplished. The best friends are those you have tested by time. They are friends chosen not only by desire, but by judgment, rather than those who enter your company through chance and intrusion. Though choosing friends is among the most important deeds in life, least care is exercised in its execution. To find pleasure in a man does not prove him a friend, for the enjoyment may spring more from the high value you set upon his company than from his capacity.

TREASURE THE WISE FRIEND

The understanding from one good friend avails you more than the good wishes of all other people in your life. One wise friend knows how to relieve you of those burdens which the fool knows only how to put upon you. But if you wish to keep this wise friend, do not overpraise him, nor be overly dependent on his abilities.

MEN OF SKILLFUL DIPLOMACY TURN INSULT TO HUMOR, FOUL PLAY TO FAIR

There are few among us who can master all the tools of diplomacy. There are men who intuitively know that even a scrap of an important man's time is not to be wasted, who have the conviction in their hearts that inspires straight talk. When a man's knowledge is deep, he speaks well of an enemy, and deals with him even better. Instead of seeking revenge, he extends unexpected generosity. In all matters, men of skillful policy turn insult into humor, turn foul play into accepted fair play, and astonish their adversaries who find no reason not to trust them. They wait, and victory comes to them. Although merit attains it, they let modesty conceal it. Such is the basis of the greatness of feeling, and the feeling of greatness.

It is a Great Feat to Make a Friend of a Rival

Foresee insult and defuse its sting, for it is less stressful to avoid insult than to avenge it. It is a great feat to make a friend of one who wished to be a rival, and to turn him into a protector of your honor when he had threatened its injury. Place him under such obligation that the insult on the tip of his tongue is turned into thanksgiving. The man who knows these secrets of life is able to transform ill will into trust. This is an art well worth learning.

CLEVERNESS IN GIVING IS TO BESTOW WHAT COSTS LITTLE BUT IS WANTED MUCH AND CHERISHED MORE

Never allow the obligation to exceed what can be repaid; for he who grants too much no longer grants, but sells. Nothing will lose more friends than to place them in too heavy debt. In order not to pay, they remove themselves from the obligation and turn into enemies. The idol does not care to be faced by the sculptor who made it, nor the debtor care to have his benefactor before his eyes. Cleverness in giving is to bestow what costs little but is wanted much, so that it is cherished more. Do good a little at a time, but often.

ATTACH YOUR VENGEANCE TO THE TIP OF A VERBAL ARROW

The situation we pursue often falls into our hands if we but stop for breath, just as the moment to avenge yourself upon your tormentor will in time present itself. Attach your vengeance to the tip of a verbal arrow, and wait. When your head is cool and your aim confident, let the arrow fly into the conscience of your badgerer. There is no better way to relieve pain caused by another than to deal with it on your terms and in your time. You will catch your antagonist unprepared for the burial of your wounds.

BE CAREFUL WHAT YOU PUT IN WRITING

It is the wise man who never defends himself with a pen, for it leaves a mark that serves more to glorify the adversary than to check him impudence. Words written and released can always be remembered, but can never be *recalled*.

THE WAY TO SILENCE
TRIVIAL MEN

It is the trick of the worthless to appear to be the opponent of great men in order to create the impression that they themselves are celebrated. There is no response better than that of ignoring these individuals. The brash try to draw attention to themselves by railing against the tyranny of the times. The way to silence trivial men is to go about your life as though they do not exist.

FEW MEN DO US GOOD, NEARLY ALL CAN DO US HARM

Among friends or enemies, never let matters come to a rupture, for you will come away from the encounter with a wounded reputation. Know that even an enemy can be of importance. Very few men do us good, but nearly all can do us harm. In the beginning of a friendship, you might have lacked prudence, in the end, patience, and many times, a good measure of common sense. These lacks spawn angry souls, glad to stir up the fire against you which has been smoldering in the hope of such an opportunity. From friends who walk in shallow waters, unable to compromise, there emerge the worst of enemies. When a parting of the ways must come, find an excuse for it. Let it be a growing coolness between friends, rather than a mounting fury between enemies. This is the well-ordered retreat.

Gracián's Recollections

THE FIFTH ENTRY:

◆

my first published books

My small room in the home of Señor and Señora Blanca faces the sun. This morning the warm, motionless air is oppressive and I feel weakened by the dampness, but my quill and parchment beckon, and my will bends to this need.

I think back to the year 1637; it was tragic in many ways. Spain was in its seventh year of war, defending the Catholic cause. Young soldiers, finding bravery in bottles of inexpensive Málaga wine, were dying in faraway places, and the war found a way to strike home.

My own personal tragedy in Belmonte, the place of my birth, bore out my father's fears and his sound reasons for long ago directing his children away from the military.

This is what I was told by my uncle Antonio, who made the long trip from Toledo to Huesca: One morning, two drunken soldiers came to my father's house pretending to need medical assistance. They soon insisted that there were hidden casks of wine on the premises. After searching but not finding any, they angrily bayoneted my beloved parents to death and escaped.

My prayers did little to console my sorrow, but I was able to find a modicum of peace when I was writing. I was completing my first novel, which I titled The Hero.

Spain, under young King Philip IV, was having problems colonizing its new territorial possessions. Its wealth was being squandered by the military, and worse, Spain was losing its dignity. There were collection boxes in the streets, and there was door-to-door soliciting for money to finance domestic incompetence and to pay for foreign defeats.

There was need for a hero: a superior man of intelligence and flawless reputation, a man who was on guard, and who was able to surmount all obstacles.

The character in my book The Hero *spoke of such obstacles. He pointed out that a river is formidable until it finds itself forded, and a man venerated until the size of his capacity is known. Intelligence and bravery are essential, but also necessary for success are concealment and prudent reserve. If the emotions are known, known also are the entrances and exits of the will, with control over it at all hours.*

The first edition of The Hero *was dedicated to Father Las-*

tanosa. When I presented the published book to him, he expressed surprise that I used the pseudonym of a deceased relative, Lorenzo Gracián, followed by the word Nobleman. I explained that it was not important that my name be on the book, only that it be published and read. My small earnings from the book were assigned to the Church; I did not seek credit, nor did I seek fame.

The other thing I did not seek, in the excitement of writing the book, was permission to publish. This provoked the new Vicar-General, who made it known to my immediate superiors that my actions were considered insolent and rebellious, and he advised them to keep a watchful eye on me.

And who was the Vicar-General? The rigid Father Segovia Montoro, who tormented me for the next twenty years as he rose in the hierarchy of the Church.

But I had my first published book, and my prayers for human dignity among men were being heard and being discussed.

Although my writing was lauded by several leaders of the Church, a letter from Father Montoro accused me of near heresy. He wrote and distributed a letter to every superior in his region as a reminder that the Church was the voice of God, that it was the Church's duty to instruct and teach, that Señor Gracián, with his false Christian name and self-proclaimed title of Nobleman, was incurring God's anger as he thrust his personal beliefs onto the pious public.

The Bishop's remarks were on the edge of accusing me of disobedience, a serious matter for an apostolic Jesuit. But this charge was not true. One who follows his conscience *cannot be judged disobedient when he reveals the Truth. My mission was to observe, to write, and to teach. It indeed was a difficult time for me, facing friends and colleagues. But I nevertheless continued to write.*

My second book, The Politician, *published two years later, was more of an essay than a full-length work. The principal character was King Ferdinand of Aragon, who lived from 1452 to 1516, and was known as the Catholic King. It was his queen Isabella, of course, who helped finance the famous expedition of Christopher Columbus in 1492.*

The Politician *described the grandeur of Spain's past, and included my studied beliefs on governing people today. As expected, I soon received Father Montoro's formal letter of criticism and admonishment, which I considered a fair exchange.*

A visit to Madrid in 1640, when I was thirty-nine years old, gave me my first look at corrupt elements in another area of our society. I had gone there for a fortnight as lecturer at the university and stayed two months. A trial that caught the country's attention was in progress, and I was among those observing the proceedings of the court's authority to interpret the law. The blatant bias of each day's proceedings validated my bitterness toward unscrupulous men in power. My observations strongly concluded that those who now judged others had not been carefully judged themselves. My written protests of court life and the legal system were circulated throughout Spain, but did little to abate the corrupt court of law.

Later that year, lecturing again, I was at the University of

Catalonia just as an upheaval was taking place. The Catalan merchants, seeking independence and avoidance of taxation, were rebelling against the central government. Inciting the people, they soon were engaged in a full-blown civil war. It was agonizing to witness brother fighting against brother, and though I personally made every effort to use my small influence for the cessation of hostilities, there was no one of reachable authority to whom I could plead my case. The number of dead increased unabated.

Returning to Huesca and to my room in the parish, I painstakingly recorded notes of what I had witnessed in Catalonia. I grieved for the youthful soldiers, the greedy merchants, and the innocent victims who found themselves caught in the melee.

As I looked beyond I saw a world in disarray and moral decline. Here, in my own parish, there was distrust among the leaders. The evil of power-seekers, even in the Church hierarchy, paralleled the self-serving ways of the wealthy landowners and devious politicians.

There were lessons to be learned and warnings to be given if survival was indeed realistic in this world.

Perhaps God had chosen me in my time to detail what I learned from all the madness about.

I learned that often the false is made to look appealing.
I learned that witnesses today may be testifiers tomorrow.
I learned that one must be careful in helping others.
I learned that you do not proclaim another man's evil.
I learned that mediocrity within yourself is unacceptable.
I learned that the more one says the less he is heard.

I learned that one does not argue with an arguer.

I learned that anonymity can be valuable.

I learned that there is safety in moving with the crowd.

I learned that not all praise is meant well.

I learned that secrets should neither be heard nor spoken.

I learned that you do not divulge what you cannot reverse.

I learned that all has its day.

THE ORACLE

Gracián On:

Lessons and Warnings

WEIGH WORDS CAREFULLY

People at cross-purposes create sparks; in the heat of an argument, when reason does not function, there lies the danger of unquenchable fires. One second of rage can cause damage that cannot be corrected in a lifetime. The craftiness of another may draw you into such a disagreement to discover where you stand, or what you think. Match this game of wiliness with determined self-restraint, especially when the argument explodes into fast repartee. Such restraint will keep you from divulging what you cannot reverse. It is true that he who knows the danger proceeds with caution. Angry words reveal little control, and words tossed out lightly can seem heavy to the one who catches them, and weighs them in his mind.

KNOW THAT THERE ARE NO SECRETS

It is the wise man who knows that he is always seen, or that he will be seen one day. He knows that walls have ears, and that what is evil breaks its shackles to be free. Even when he is alone he works as though the eyes of the world are upon him, because he knows that everything comes to be known. He knows that those who hear his thoughts today are witnesses and can be testifiers tomorrow. So he lives by the rules of private thoughts. He knows that when he gives up the smallest part of a secret, the rest is no longer in his power. In this manner he is well prepared for confrontation, and in control of what becomes public.

ONLY THE SINS OF LITTLE-KNOWN PEOPLE ARE LITTLE KNOWN

It is a sign of weakness in yourself to point a finger at the shame of another. Some seek to whitewash their own stains with the blotches of others, and in this manner console themselves. But the odor of the breath is foul from these diggers of the sewer's filth. And he who digs deepest, soils himself most. Few are free from some sin of their own, be it of commission or omission. For only the sins of little-known people are little known. Let the man who is alert in the ways of the world guard against being a recorder of evil, for in doing so he becomes a man to be despised. Reporting the sin of another leaves a permanent stain on the conscience of your own mind.

KNOW YOUR OWN WEAKNESSES

man's failings live in the spirit of himself. Even the man most perfect does not escape having some weakness, and more often than not, he is not blind to these failings, because he loves them. Weaknesses tolerated by others who do not see, or choose not to see, give false approval to the owner of these shallow traits. Unfortunately, the majority of men strike at once upon these shortcomings, and finding them offensive, find joy in seeing the owner make a fool of himself. Know your pet failings and be willing to let go of them. Here is an opportunity for self-betterment that will make the best of your best qualities shine forth more brightly.

SEEK SAFETY IN ANONYMITY

Avoid labels, especially self-acclaimed ones, for when they alone identify you, even your distinctions can become defects. Labels stem from peculiarity, which always raises questions. Even beauty, when too outstanding, is blinding, just as one cannot look directly at the sun. Whatever attracts notice is open to offense and criticism, even revenge from false friends and envious strangers. Beware of the man who seeks prominence in villainy, hunting for distinction in notoriety. When he achieves his goal he will vie to entangle others for his own profit and respectability. The thrust of such men will not be subtle, and therefore one can prepare. The golden rule is: Before you step into the foreground with another, examine the background. The wise man who accomplishes much collects his reward and allows his subordinates to collect the credit. There is a large measure of safety in anonymity.

Not all praise is well meant

There are those with low self-esteem who address all things with malice. Their "yes" means "no" and their "no" means "yes." The opposite is constantly to be inferred, and everything is turned about. To minimize something means they have a high regard for it. To gain something for themselves, they will cheapen it before others. Not all praise is well meant, for some praise the evil in order not to praise the good. Their perversity is counteractive, and those in their presence would best acknowledge them with blind eyes and deaf ears.

Know how to plead your case

*T*here is an art to pleading a case whether you entreat, implore, or beseech. Yet, there is nothing more difficult for some, and nothing easier for others. It is essential to know with whom you deal. There are those who do not know how to refuse, and with such men it is not necessary to be a trickster. There are others to whom "no" is always the first word, and at any hour. Catch them when recently refreshed in body or spirit, and when their attention has not already been awakened to your motives. Do not approach the donor when another man has just been turned away, for at that moment "no" is still rampant. Prior to pleading your case, discover the donor's weakness, the topics that relax him, and use this as your entry point. But do not think him stupid if he bends to this subterfuge, as you cannot presume to interpret his mood or read his mind. You will gain your end, provided, of course, that you are not dealing with a villain. Note that if you have previously placed the other under obligation to you, the transaction is merely a trade.

THE GLITTER OF GLASS BELIES ITS WEAKNESS

*T*he false in everything is made to look appealing. Thus the false is forever in the lead, continually dragging along the fools. The truth lags behind, waiting for the man of insight to seize it for advantage of the situation at hand. Look beneath. For ordinarily things are not what they seem. The person who does not seek to pass beyond the surface is quickly disillusioned if he gets deeper into the interior. The superficial are taken in at once. The man of substance lives safely within himself, and is treasured by his colleagues.

THE MORE SAID, THE LESS HEARD

The man versed in one topic, who pursues one line of reason, and makes only one long speech, is apt to be boring. Brevity charms and accomplishes the daily course of events; it makes up in manner what it lacks in measure. The good, if short, is doubly good, and the bad, if brief, is only half as bad. As in wine, the essence is always stronger than the dregs. It is commonly perceived that the man long-winded in rhetoric is rarely wise. The more he says, the less is heard, for what is well said is said quickly. There are men who cannot refrain from making themselves a nuisance, even in the company of the most accomplished who are much occupied. They never learned that the time allotted to a great man is more precious than gold. To impose on such a man is unforgiveable.

NOT ALL WHO LOOK, SEE

not all who see, see with open eyes, and so they see not all. To see too late does not bring help, and may only bring grief. Some start seeing when there is no longer anything to see, when the tangible that was invisible to them is suddenly removed. Will and understanding sharpen the vision. To instill understanding in one who has no will is a difficult task. Even more difficult is to instill will in one who has no understanding. Those who comprehend the ways of the world dance around these individuals as if they were blind and deaf. These lost individuals, at constant disadvantage, are a source of amusement, but there is no lack of unscrupulous men to encourage this blindness to reality; such unprincipled louts thrive because others look but do not see.

DO NOT DIE OF ANOTHER'S MISERY

Beware of those mired in misfortune who call to you for comfort. These men are on the hunt for those who will help them carry their baggage of adversity. You hear from them intermittently, yet they have no twinge of conscience about asking for a helping hand. Know that these men cleverly maintain relationships with the soft-hearted, even those whom they have bluffed and cheated in the past. Great coolness is necessary with the drowning if you would bring them help without peril to yourself.

BEWARE THE PITFALLS OF PITY

The world is such that one who is disliked when he prospers is adored in times of adversity. The hatred for the exalted man changes to sympathy when he is cast down. Let the observer of human behavior take note of how the cards of fortune are shuffled. Never through pity for another's unhappiness ought one to involve himself in the lot of the unfortunate. Recognize that one could never be lucky if many others were not unlucky. Some unfortunates become faithful followers of those who wish to make recompense by senseless charity. They imagine there are benefits to be gained by winning the favor of the affluent who wish to be surrounded by others' gratitude, praise, and approval. This strange union produces mostly words, seldom deeds.

THE NOVELTY OF THE NEW IS SHORT-LIVED

*T*here is a measure of excitement in the new, be it possessions or people. For as long as you are deemed new, you rate high. Novelty fares well because it is different, it refreshes the senses. At times brand-new mediocrity is more cherished than shopworn perfection. Even the best of things become boring. But note that the glory of the new is short-lived, and that in a matter of days or weeks all respect for it will fade. Therefore, know to make use of the time of approval. For when the fire of the new is spent, fervor cools, and the excitement for the young, or the new, will be exchanged for the comfort, sometimes the boredom, of the old. Believe then that everything has its day, and also that it passes.

NEVER SHARE IN YOUR SUPERIOR'S SECRETS

never participate in the secrets of those above you. You think you are privileged to share the fruit, but you also may be sharing the pits and the rind, and you run the risk of being eaten. In sharing secrets you unwittingly become the mirror of private matters carelessly revealed, and many have broken the mirror that reminded them of their ugliness. He who tells his secrets to another makes himself that man's slave, and this is a strain that cannot be tolerated, especially by those who rule. Feeling imprisoned by a revealed secret they wish to retract, they will trample upon everything, even justice, to achieve this goal. When friends become enemies, secrets shared in time of lightness become poisoned arrows dipped in vengeance. Secrets, therefore, should never be heard, and never spoken.

LET HIM WHO KNOWS LITTLE, SAY LITTLE

In the work force, whatever his job, let him who knows little, say little, and in this manner stay on the safe side. Even though he is not adjudged smart, he will be adjudged sound. He who is professionally trained to make business judgments may let his imagination roam, but he who knows little and takes chances voluntarily tries suicide. Hold always to the proven, for what is established as right cannot be wrong. The road you travel is fixed, and therefore proven, and the right of way is law for everybody. There is safety in moving with the crowd.

LEAVE ROOM FOR A SECOND IMPRESSION

Some men are easily impressed. The first story they hear may in itself be fabricated, and since the lie always pushes itself out in front, it leaves little room for the truth to gain attention. Neither our wish for what we have first observed nor our sympathy for the first heard should so fill us with conclusions that we find ourselves at our capacity of acceptance. Whether it be naïveté or inflexibility, some men are like new casks which forever retain the smell of the first liquor poured into them, be it bad or good. When this shortsightedness comes to be known, it can be fatal, for it fails to defend against those of evil intent. In all situations, leave room for a second impression; save space for the second and even the third report, not allowing your opinions to border on the too passionate.

DO NOT ARGUE WITH AN ARGUER

There are those so contrary that arguing is second nature. Therefore, when there is little to be won, there is much to avoid. Know that all such confrontations cannot be totally shunned and, finding yourself immersed, decide whether the argument springs from astuteness or from foul disposition. Sometimes it is not pigheadedness but a trick. Pay heed, therefore, not to entangle yourself in the one, while you play the game of disentangling yourself from the other. There are those who are called lock-pickers of the soul. The thrust of their arguments is to enrage and weaken the opponent. There is no better counter-trick than to leave the key of caution in the lock.

THERE IS DANGER IN COMPLACENCY

Self-satisfaction should not be displayed or voiced, for there is no joy in it for anyone else. On the other hand, to be unsatisfied with yourself implies a lack of courage. Self-complacency starts for the most part in wit-lessness and ends in a blissful ignorance which, even though soothing to the soul, does not inspire respect from others. Even if you are unable to equal the qualifications of great men, do not find reasons to live with mediocrity within yourself. It is always more useful and more intelligent to have misgivings about yourself, either for your better assurance that things will come off well, or for your better comfort if they come off badly. It is said that he cannot be surprised by mishaps, or by a turn of luck, who has already feared it. Complacency, unchecked, grows and grows, sowing seeds, and therein lies its danger.

AVOID BEING A COMPLAINER

*T*he need to release frustration makes a perfectly pleasant man a lamentable bore. Never cry about your woes; it only discredits you. Because problems pass and people remember, it is less regrettable to be timid in the outpouring of complaints. In politics, many a man with his protest of past injustices has invited additional problems by crying for help or expecting pity. It is far better to praise the generosity of one than to complain about a score of others; this invites further generosities. Reciting the favors done for you by those who are absent extracts and identifies them from those who are present; this calls others' attention to the esteem in which you are held. And so a man of good sense will never make known to the world the slights or the wrongs he may have suffered, but only the honor in which he is held.

Do not condemn what the crowd applauds

Be careful in condemning what pleases many; it must contain some good to be so satisfying to the public, even though it cannot be explained to your satisfaction. The man who stands apart, out of stubbornness or ignorance, is watching opportunity passing by. His business acumen is suspect, and his judgment is discredited, and he is likely to be left alone in his poor taste. If you do not know how to profit from the good, conceal your blindness, and do not condemn in wholesale fashion. Bad choice is ordinarily the child of ignorance. What the masses embrace, be it trend or novel, is reality for the moment.

GRACIÁN'S RECOLLECTIONS

THE SIXTH ENTRY:

◆

REWARDS OF MATURITY

𝒞his morning I found six sharpened goose feather quills lying neatly across my small desk, and my inkwell filled to the brim. Señora Blanca, who cannot read or write, exceeded the meaning of kindness to provide the necessary tools for me to do so. What would I do without her?

And warmed by the spirit of her caring, I move my pen now back to the year 1642. To my surprise, not once did I hear from Father Montoro, even though the texts of my sermons were being reported to him. In Barcelona, he had recently been appointed Archbishop, and I judged that perhaps he was too occupied to think much of me. But in my mind, his stern face and narrow eyes stood over me like the blade of a guillotine.

My good fortune began that year when I was offered the position of Vice-Rector of the Jesuit House of Probation in Tarragona. Never did I imagine that this small northeastern city would have meaning in my later life, for it was at Tarragona that I first became aware of Señor and Señora Blanca.

Whenever I raised my eyes from the pulpit I would find them seated in their front-row pew, listening attentively. I learned from a priest that this pious couple, who had recently relocated from Graus, had a small, modest home several miles from the parish, a sturdy horse and carriage, and that they never missed attending Sunday morning mass.

During my tenure at Tarragona I often noticed one of the monks jotting down portions of my sermons. I was certain that this information was reported to Bishop Montoro. This covert action was also observed by my immediate Superior, Father Olivares, who, almost as a gesture of defiance, expressed his confidence by recommending me for the higher position of confessor and preacher at the novitiate in Valencia.

So it was with sadness that I bade farewell to the Blancas. I recall saying to them, rather prophetically, that if it was God's will, we would meet again.

Valencia, 1644. St. Ignatius Church was marked by young, rowdy parishioners who scoffed at working, and berated anyone who attempted to instruct them in good manners. It was not above this vulgar group, seated among serious worshipers, to whistle loudly and, from time to time, hurl garden vegetables at the priest and the choir. It was shameful.

I viewed this new position not only as an advancement in my career but as a personal challenge in dealing with a difficult situation. I devised a plan for my first appearance in the pulpit.

With my eyes fastened on the ringleader, I began: "Good people and parishioners of St. Ignatius Church of Valencia, I have before me a letter which I shall read to you. This letter was sent from Hell."

The audience gasped. A moment later my mock congratulatory note praising the evildoers in Satan's service caused hostility such as I have never witnessed. Docile parishioners became so enraged at the ruffians who cheered and applauded my fictitious letter that they literally fell upon them with canes, crutches, sticks, and bare fists to drive them into the street. Many of them were bleeding and others, being grossly outnumbered, were pleading for mercy.

I received a humorous congratulatory letter from the popular dramatist, Calderón de la Barca. I also received a somber visit from my immediate superior, who, acting on a directive from Archbishop Montoro, was forced to place me under house restraint. My privileges and preachings were suspended for a fortnight, and no one was permitted to speak to me. My personal letters were withheld, and I was fed once a day.

Later, I learned that the rowdies did not return to church

the following Sunday, and the few who did attend after this incident sat quietly and respectfully.

The two years (1644–1646) I spent in Valencia were difficult but rewarding. When I left St. Ignatius, order had been fully restored, and my immediate superior embraced me.

Huesca, the beginning of the year, 1646. Returning to my home parish and to long candlelight hours of writing, I completed what some critics considered a controversial book. I called it The Discreet Man. *I readily admit that I was influenced by the aggressive element in our midst, and that the work contained fragments of cynical views of mankind. But it also contained a treasury of traditional values and spiritual truths which needed to be embraced, and these I strongly urged.*

I requested and received permission to publish The Discreet Man, *but permission arrived with a harsh addendum. I was instructed to stop further writing and publishing. The threat was clear: If I disobeyed, there would be consequences.*

However, at that moment, writing was not absorbing my thoughts. The beautiful city of Lérida had come under siege by the French, and I hastily volunteered as chaplain to the army under Don Diego Felipe de Guzman.

I found myself in the midst of furious battles. The agony of young faces smeared with their own blood is too painful to detail. In the throes of such devastation, personal fear was inconsequential, and I take no pride in having been acclaimed the Priest of Victory. Death, even the death of our enemies in victory, is brutal. Some said I behaved fearlessly.

It is not entirely true. I only did what I was there to do, to give comfort to the wounded and dying.

The year 1646 ended in despair for me. Unrest and lack of civility worsened. Riots in the streets were a daily occurrence, and there were fires burning everywhere. The decline of the Spanish Empire seemed unstoppable. Yet everyday life and everyday business affairs continued for most.

As the sadness of the nation increased, so did the number of parishioners. In my sermons, I prayed that they find a way to muster the reserve of strength that we closet in our hearts for troubled times. And in my prayer to Saint Catherine of Siena, my plea was to "obtain the grace not only to pass unscathed through the corruption of this world, but also to remain unshakably faithful to the Church, in work, in deed, in example, to see always, and to make others see . . . the beacon light that points the way to the harbor of safety in the dark night of our times and of men's souls."

Although I constantly spoke of hope, faith, tolerance, and courage, among other topics, I never failed to stress the basic survival tool, common sense.

One should always know the way the wind is blowing.
One should not let feelings overwhelm good judgment.
One should know to leave before being left.
One should not give time to a contradictory man.
One should not too quickly bend to the spirit of the moment.
One should know when to reveal and when to conceal.
One should know when to walk the middle road.

One should accumulate a collection of favors owed.
One should always deal with men of honor.
One should know when to arrive and when to exit.

In essence, I urged people to seek inner guidance to reach clear conclusions as a way to go on with their lives in these troubled times.

Although I grow weaker each day, the themes of those small sermons remain fresh in my mind. The human brain is truly miraculous.

THE ORACLE

Gracián On:

common sense decisions

WALK THE MIDDLE ROAD

No one and nothing today is in agreement. Intelligent writers present profound essays which we praise, only to find ourselves at another time praising another belief on the same topic that is just as convincing. We emotionally respond to ideas that match our moods so that at times we are discontent when our fortune is at its best and content in our minds when our fortune couldn't be worse. Our pendulum of moods sometimes makes us unhappy with our lot, only to see joy in someone else's. And there are those who believe that the past is better, and glorify only the things of yesterday. Better to walk the middle road, for it is to be concluded that he is just as much a fool who laughs at everything as is he who weeps at everything.

EXIT GRACEFULLY

Know how to make a triumph of your exit. The graceful exit at the propitious moment is a victory in itself. At times the sun herself, at its brightest, will retire behind a cloud so that she may not be seen, leaving us to wonder and long for her return. Do not wait until men turn their backs upon you, until they bury you, still alive in your feelings but dead in their estimation. The man of foresight puts his inferior horse in the stable early, and does not wait to see it create shock by falling in the middle of the race. The beautiful woman wisely cracks her mirror when it is yet early in her life, so as not to smash it with impatience later when it has disillusioned her. A maxim for the wise: Leave before being left.

Beware the Whims of Human Behavior

It can be dispiriting to observe the dark side of man. Half the world laughs at the other half, even though the lot are all fools. Either everything is good or everything is bad, depending on the whim of the moment. What one will refuse, another pursues, for there are as many minds as there are heads, and as different. An insufferable fool is he who wishes the universe to be governed according to his plans. Weakness has its own admirers, and if certain ways of living displease some, they will not fail to please others. Yet the opposite is also true: Let approval of your strengths make you vain and there are others waiting to condemn you. In truth, proper satisfaction may be taken only in the approval of men of true wisdom, and by those who have standing in their fields. Do not live by the approval of any one voice, or of any one custom, or of any single period in time.

DO NOT PLAY TO LOSE

For some, failure is a way of life. Having started down the wrong road, they think it a badge of character to be consistent. They admit their error to their inner selves, but to those in the outer world who will listen, they readily offer reasons and excuses that validate their actions. To this end they are marked pathetic fools, as they go about slowly starving the roots of life. They should know neither impulsive promise nor wrong resolve are binding upon any man, and yet some will on this account continue in their sulkiness, and carry on in their contrariness, as though being constant in their idiocies proves their strength of character.

NEVER EXHIBIT YOUR WORK HALF-DONE

s all beginnings are without form, and the image of this shapelessness endures in the imagination, undertakings are to be enjoyed only when complete. Early stages of work when viewed by others leaves a memory of imperfection. Later, the same memory transfers itself into the completed project. By having been divided into two images of reference, memory forbids the enjoyment of the magnificence in one gaze; it blurs the judgment of final details. Before an object is everything, it is nothing. In its inception, it is still very close to being nothing. Recognize that the sight of preparation of even the daintiest morsel may turn more people to disgust than to appetite. Whatever your creative work, see to it that it not be shown in embryo form. Learn from nature herself not to bring it forth until it is ready to be seen.

DO NOT YIELD TO THE LATEST RUMOR

Some men are forever carried away by the last news they hear, which makes them go to ridiculous extremes in the decisions that follow. They are as soft and as impressionable as wax, and therefore always bend to the event of the moment. Because they lack vision, the final news replaces all preceding events. In commerce, the last price will frighten such a man into buying, believing the cost will rise, whereas the sophisticated buyer waits, or finds a substitute that has held steady. The nervous traders, so mobile, never stay put, every man tinting them with his own color. They are a poor choice as partners and confidants, and remain children all their lives. And like children, they are ever changing in spirit and feelings, and perpetually in a state of flux.

DO NOT REVEAL EVERYTHING

neither be all nor give all to anyone, for there is a big difference between the bestowal of your affection and the bestowal of yourself, and the closest of ties and the laws of intimacy must not be exceptions. Something should always be kept hidden, even from a friend, and something concealed even from a father by his son. Certain secrets are kept from the one and imparted to the other, and vice versa. It is said that almost everything is revealed, or almost everything is concealed, depending upon whom one is with.

ENJOY A LITTLE MORE, STRIVE A LITTLE LESS

Men driven by ambition often succeed outwardly and fail inwardly. Their outer resources multiply at the cost of their spiritual energy. Yet they go blindly forward with small consideration that happy leisure is worth more than drive; for nothing belongs to us except time. Precious existence is squandered in stupid drudgery. Overwork is the mother of greed and the substitute for boredom. Once entrapped, escape comes only with the slow collapse of body functions. So be not crushed under success, and be not be crushed under envy! To be so is to trample upon life and to suffocate the spirit. Enjoy a little more, strive a little less. The wise man will extend his life's work to prolong his life.

LEARN HOW TO USE FAVORS

In the world of business, always deal with men of honor so that your favors are not wasted; you can then employ the politician's knack of doing a needed favor before it is earned. The favor thus advanced has double merit. The casual manner in which it is bestowed lays greater obligation upon him who receives it. The politician uses this as a stepping-stone to heighten his career. Though he may not always be loved, he has no shortage of friends who are happy to be on the receiving end of his good graces, and even happier to make restitution when called upon. Favors constitute promissory notes which are collectible at the donor's convenience. Timed correctly, the collection of favors can yield handsome profits. But this is true only between men with a sense of honor. With mean-minded men, advance payment of a pledge acts more as a restraint than as a responsibility.

OUTSHINE YOUR PREDECESSOR

Be on guard when you are chosen to fill a position higher than the one you previously held. It is a hard task to fill a great gap, for what has gone before always appears better. Even doing equally as well does not suffice, because the one who preceded you holds the prior claim. If you commit yourself to such a situation, let it be in the knowledge that you have command of additional gifts which will dispossess the other of the higher opinion in which he is held. For it will be necessary to be worth double merely to equal your predecessor. Likewise, when the time comes for your replacement, it is wise to see to it that he who succeeds you is such that you are the one who is missed, praised in remembrance, and wished back.

TEST THE WIND

*T*esting out the public temper and learning where you stand is essential in law, in industry, and in government, for it is not enough to be right if you have a malicious face and others bear you malice. In a new enterprise or innovation, know which way the wind is blowing. Early warning helps one discover how a matter will later be received. Whether you expect its success or sanction, you gain assurance of its final outcome by canvassing opinions, collecting hard-fisted facts, and understanding the leaning of your own intuition. Then you will discover if you must go forward or turn back.

LEARN THE ART OF ELOQUENCE

Strangely, most men have low regard for what they understand, and respect only what is beyond them. They honor most what they cannot grasp. Many give praise, but if asked why, can give no reason. For they revere all that is mysterious, and they sing its praises because they hear its praises sung. In doing business make a strong effort to appear a little wiser and smarter, properly and not excessively, in order to command respect. It is true that with men of understanding wisdom counts for everything, but for the majority refining your speaking skills will help you complete a transaction. Shrewd businessmen know that accomplished oratory will keep buyers and sellers off guard by engaging them in the mere business of interpretation, allowing no time for criticism.

FIT YOURSELF TO THE FRAMEWORK OF YOUR WORLD

Live as best you can in the state of affairs that surrounds you. Wish for what is available, work at what is achievable. Yet do not always journey through life by the laws written to regulate you, even when such laws have the face of righteousness and goodness. Take small liberties and byways without bringing harm to yourself and to others. Do not indicate too precisely what alone will satisfy you, for tomorrow your words may have to be disregarded. Stay flexible and be alert as the days change and new opportunities arise. There are some so unreasonable that they would have every circumstance of life fit itself into their own framework when it should be the other way around. The man of wisdom knows better: he lives as best as he can in the state of affairs that surrounds him.

If you would lead, let others take responsibility for errors

It is the wise strategy of those who govern, in state or industry, to carry a shield against vicious ill will pledged against them. They must know how to let the responsibility for something amiss rest upon another. It is not a mark of weakness, as the envious think, but of greater strength to have on hand someone to bear the brunt for failure in order to continue to govern without hindrance. Weigh the situation at hand. It may be a wise business decision to let someone atone for your errors even though it cost you some of your pride. Self-preservation is at the heart of survival. Not everything can come off well, nor everyone be satisfied.

EXAMINE BOTH SIDES OF A DISAGREEMENT

Know that every man believes according to his own interests, and that he is filled with reasons and excuses for his stand. In most instances feeling overwhelms judgment and passion takes hold. Thus two opinions confront each other and each man believes that his is the side of reason. But reason, always fair, cannot be two-faced. The man of good sense treads cautiously in so delicate a situation. He allows the possibility of misgivings in his own mind to moderate his judgment regarding that of the other. At that moment he lets his imagination stray to the opposite position. There he can examine the arguments of both sides, seeing what is so puzzling and exasperating to two well-intended people, who may in addition be two misguided idealists.

DO NOT DUEL WITH A CONTRARY MAN

Cut short conversations where someone continuously contradicts himself for the sake of prolonging an argument. This reveals gross obstinacy. A bickering disputant cannot escape being marked the fool, for he makes warfare of quiet talk, and so becomes an enemy to his friends. In most conversations, expressing an opposite view may prove an opponent to be clever, but much depends on its limits. At a certain point, stretching his contrariness can only lead him to the dunce's cap. Understand that the contrary man finds perverse joy in creating an atmosphere of cruelty. If you find yourself in such a corner, play silent. Give your combatant no one with whom to duel, and the sword will fall lamely from his hand.

USELESS DISCUSSIONS NEVER LEAD TO USEFUL DECISIONS

*T*here are those who discuss a single point over and over, wearying themselves and wearying others, yet never arrive at the heart of the matter. They are the people who grope for random answers in the wind, hoping to snare a solution that will meet with the approval of their opponent. It matters little to them if they themselves agree with the justification, just as long as the person opposite does. This, they believe, will earn them respect and confidence. Such men spend time and exhaust patience over questions they should leave alone. If the situation is important to you, play the role of compromiser. Put yourself in the middle, consider all the points of the argument to arrive at a solution. Settle the matter, but know that the less people think the more they talk, and that useless discussions never lead to useful decisions.

MAKE INTELLIGENCE THE FOUNDATION OF YOUR LIFE

Be the architect of your life. Know how to arrange it with intelligence, not as accident may dictate. Plant its foundation firmly, and develop it with foresight. Know that life is a difficult, fatiguing expedition without recreation, much like a long journey without inns in which to refresh and rejuvenate oneself. Intellectual stimulation mixes well with the dust and stones of the long road to eternity. We are born to know the world and to know ourselves, and the great books of truth make us into men. Therefore, spend a period of your life in the company of the venerated thinkers and writers of the past. But spend the mainstream of your life with the living in order to see and to note all the good that is upon this earth. Know that everything is not to be found in one region; the omnipotent Father has divinely divided His blessing and has, at times, adorned the ugliest in the richest coverlets. Let the remainder of your life be wholly your own. To live in the mind and explore the tributaries of philosophy is the ultimate good fortune of man.

GRACIÁN'S RECOLLECTIONS

THE SEVENTH ENTRY:

◆

the writing comes of age

J awakened feeling strong and energetic, and I feel urged to write at a greater pace.

Perhaps, it is because in these recollections I have come to the most energetic period of my life.

I was living in Huesca in 1647. I was forty-six years old, and it was a time when my writings and sermons seemed to come of age. It was a period of such creative intensity that a day of writing seemed only twenty minutes long.

The reason for this accelerated motivation was undoubt-

edly a new patron who also became a dear personal friend. My new patron had a poetic name and a friendly face. He was Don Pablo de Parada, an admirable Portuguese noble-man and soldier, now retired. He had no family of his own, and was a giving, compassionate friend to the poor.

This was a drastic change from my earlier support, which had come from a mysterious unidentified gentleman whom I referred to as Señor Donador. When his messenger first approached me, he revealed only that a kindly old gentle-man, after hearing me speak, wished to support the publi-cation of my writings. The money would go to the monks and the friars who earned their living by printing the works of authors such as myself. This unknown patron, Señor Donador, lent his support for many years. One day I was informed that he had died. I never did discover his true identity, although he could have been any one of many peo-ple who supported my humanistic views.

My collaboration with Señor de Parada began in an un-usual way. He lived in Huesca, attended Sunday services, and had a penchant for taking notes on my extemporane-ous sermons. After several months we met, at which time he sincerely urged me to think of organizing these notes into the "rules of life," as he called them, and, of course, add to them. I did not have a project in progress, and his "rules of life" presented a genuine challenge to me. Know-ing that a writer cannot exist without a sponsor, Señor de Parada graciously volunteered to support the project.

The book, entitled The Manual Oracle, *and the* Art of Pru-dence, *was completed in 1648, and it remains, in my heart, the most important work of my life. Señor de Parada did not* approve of my using the pseudonym Lorenzo Gracián, but I convinced him that the credit of authorship was of little importance to me; more important was readership. He was a softhearted man and he did not oppose me.

The work, for sale in university libraries and sometimes from a stall in front of a church, was an instant success. So much so that a buyer would have to wait his turn to purchase a copy. Because of the shortage of books it was not unusual for the owner to invite a group of friends to his home, where he would read aloud from the book and the group would discuss topic after topic far into the night.

Señor de Parada and I were overjoyed with our first collaboration. Whispered words of praise came from many Jesuit friends.

But Archbishop Montoro viewed the success of the book as a further blight on my "dubious character." As a final mark of his disdain, he ordered the printers to discontinue assembling copies of this "useless information to the unprotected public."

The Oracle might have been quickly forgotten had there not been a sanctified visit from my wartime friend, General Don Diego Felipe de Guzman, brother of the chief minister to the King. Yes, he had read The Oracle and he had heard about my problems with the Bishop. His astonishing message that afternoon was that King Philip IV had expressed interest in meeting privately with me in his palace. No reason was given.

An invitation of this sort was unheard of. I accepted immediately, and two days later I was ushered into a large, majestically ornamented room where the young, casually *dressed King stood up and greeted me with warmth and friendliness. It is a moment that I shall never forget.*

We spoke of many things. The tall, handsome monarch was unusually articulate for his age and particularly progressive in the field of arts and letters. At one point he shared his poetry with me, asking my opinion of this line and that line. Later, to my surprise, he reached for a copy of The Politician, *the eulogy to Ferdinand the Catholic which I had written seven years earlier. It became the topic of our discussion. King Philip appeared to be singularly interested in my "observations and advice" regarding the perfect ruler.*

It was not the topic that I would have chosen to discuss. I remember the King saying, "Ah, so you have taken it upon yourself to instruct present and future generations." His good-natured laugh indicated that he did not find this notion offensive. Perhaps he did not take it seriously.

After several hours in his presence, and just as I was preparing to depart, he reached for his copy of The Oracle, *waved it several times in the air, and said: "I will have a serious word with the Archbishop."*

Thus with pressure and threats abated, I was able, in the following years, to complete various works that were well received by the critics and the public. However, what lifted my spirit most of all was the continued demand for the "rules of life" contained in The Oracle.

I remember a young priest from a nearby parish arriving one afternoon at the conclusion of a class that I was teaching. He was clutching a copy of the book. One of the essays touched on a problem that was affecting his life. In short, he hoped that I could help him overcome his tendency toward vanity and self-centeredness. This chronic obsession of being concerned solely with his own needs weighed heavily on his heart.

I invited him to attend the next class I was teaching. In place of my regular lecture I substituted a discussion of "The Conceited Man," one of the small sermons in The Oracle.

A general round of debate on the subject lasted for several hours, and endless ideas sprang from the minds of the students. The grateful young priest, amazed at the alternatives, blissfully departed with a fresh outlook and a new understanding of his problem. It was an exhilarating day.

I have a sound reason for mentioning this small incident. Perhaps upon reading "The Conceited Man," as well as the other writings herein, you, too, will meet with a group of colleagues of equal intelligence to discuss these topics and make the findings your own.

Intelligence is your guiding star for the journey you choose in life. The difference between a wise decision and a foolish one can sometimes be no more than the small light ignited by a single thought. Knowing what is wise is the key to survival.

It is wise to know that a man will never be enriched by envy.

It is wise not to seek the answer before the question has been fully heard and understood.

It is wise to know that all that is natural is always more pleasing.

It is wise to join the crowd, but know your place.
It is wise to know the nature of the beast.
It is wise to know when to yield a point.
It is wise to be clothed in tasteful thinking.
It is wise to befriend a man of spiritual substance.
It is wise to control the random ravings of the mind.
It is wise to do at once what a fool does last.

T H E   O R A C L E

Gracián On:

Wise men and fools

WISE MEN NEVER KNOW ENOUGH

Whereas mental starvation is catastrophic to the wise, too much thinking and too much counsel suffocate the fool; mental fatigue claims him without a blow being struck. Some men die because they have sense; others live because they have none. Learning is life to the wise and slow death to the fool. The wise man never knows enough and will only offer advice when asked; the fool believes he knows too much and has advice for anyone who will listen. However, both fool and wise man fall victim when the nourishing of their respective needs becomes excessive.

BEWARE OF THOSE WHO WALK UNDER A DARK CLOUD

There are men who, early in life, develop a side in their nature so dark that they are incapable of savoring the sunshine. They find comfort in being alone and stay withdrawn even from those who care the most about them. This sad quirk of nature makes them condemn everyone, some for what they have done, and others for what they may do. Victims of their own pendulum of moods, such men are either deadly quiet or accuse with ferociousness, for in their excitement, they push everything to extremes. They live in a palace one day, a prison the next. Emotionally frozen, they are a terror to many, but mostly to themselves. In desperation they reach for those born with softness, and their greatest challenge is to sustain this delicate relationship. But most fail because they do not learn to let the cloud go by.

JOIN THE CROWD, BUT KNOW YOUR PLACE

Be not always the lead nor always the clown in an attempt to play the important role. Seeking admiration from others may result in silent derision. Some momentary concession may be made to gain popularity, but never go further than the crowd goes. For he who is counted the fool in public will not be regarded as discreet in private. More may be lost in one day of foolery than can be regained in a lifetime of seriousness. But by the same token, do not forever stand apart, for to do so is to appear critical and condemn the others.

THE CONCEITED MAN HAS FEW REAL FRIENDS

Hear what others have to say. To listen only to your own voice is nonsense. To wish to listen to yourself, and this before others, is nonsense twice over. It is small comfort to be satisfied with yourself if you do not satisfy others, and a general feeling of contempt usually punishes such conceit. To be the speaker and a member of the audience too does not sit well. It is the habit of conceited gentlemen to speak in terms of "I this" and "I that" and be so carried away by the sound of their own voice that they are impervious to the torture their words inflict on those who must listen. Inflated men always mouth other men's words, and as their talk parades through the ranks of ignorance, there is always some fool who nods approval and says, "Well said!"

Think Before Voicing Complaints

There are those who constantly offend the sensitivities of others, and always foolishly. They drift into a crowd with ease, but they part with difficulty, having quickly worn out their welcome. No day is complete for them without its hundred annoyances. They put their understanding on the wrong side of the discussion and find fault with everything. Unable to do anything right themselves, they call the efforts of others wrong. A constant embarrassment to themselves and to others, it has never occurred to them that to think before uttering a negative word provides the power to control the random ravings of the mind.

THE MAN WHO TALKS TOO MUCH

What is on his mind is on his tongue, and the tongue is a beast, which, once at large, is hard to recapture and chain. Acting on the pulse of the soul, enraptured by the beat of the spirit, he who should be most restrained is often the least. His penchant for being heard overrides the consequences. He listens not, and hears little when he does. His mind seeks the answer before the question has been sprung, and inevitably he is wrong. Opinionated beyond tolerance, he is forced to seek a new audience daily, as few wish to receive his barrage of nonsense more than once. If he had the capacity to listen, someone in the path of his repartee would whisper to him that man, in order to prove how much he is the master of himself, does not get himself constantly stirred up or involved in everything that crosses his mind.

THE WISE MAN DOES AT ONCE WHAT THE FOOL DOES LAST

A wise man quickly evaluates each step and moves with confidence. A fool follows his basic instincts although they have often led him astray. He who starts confused continues in this style ever after, unaware that his internal compass, incorrectly aligned, is prescribing false directions. Not until he arrives does he know that he is where he had not intended to be. If you desire to correct this lack of navigational skill, you must attach yourself to a proven captain without disclosing your blunderings. Note that the man of sense instantly recognizes what sooner or later must be, and does it to his joy and to his credit; he does at once what a fool does last. The wise man and the fool do the same thing, only at different times: the first in season, the second out of season.

BE PREPARED FOR EVERY KIND OF FOOL

Go prepared, always, against the discourteous, the stubborn, the presumptuous, and every kind of fool. One encounters many, and intelligence lies in avoiding all of them. Before the mirror of your watchfulness, arm yourself daily with resolution on this point, and thus be prepared against foolish accident. The man forearmed with intelligence will not be engaged by impertinence. The way is difficult through this human sea, for it is filled with rocks upon which merely standing upright entertains the possibility of capsizing. To sail around them is safest. Of great value in all these matters is a feigned blindness. Cover everything with the cloak of courtesy, for that is the quick and quiet way out of all embarrassments.

DO NOT OVERREACT TO JESTS

In the world of business, one must know how to be on the receiving end of those brief narratives that provoke laughter; receiving them is a kind of gallantry, but playing them is a way into difficulty. A humorous anecdote enlivens. Let him who is piqued show no irritation toward the one who piqued him. Better yet, he should take little notice, and safest of all is to let it pass. The mood of light enjoyment often turns dark and sometimes brutal when overreaction to humor surfaces. At times like these, avoid prolonging the situation; there is nothing that demands greater skill. And when you are the jester, know exactly to what point of sufferance you will be driving your subject before you begin.

STUBBORNNESS LOSES THE ARGUMENT

*T*here is pride so foolish that it clings to stubbornness, right or wrong. The problem with this miserable trait deepens when the characteristic persists, for there is far greater harm in stubborn actions than in talk. In a general debate, the wise man seizes the better side of the argument, whereas the fool, now entrapped, defends the wrong side out of obstinacy. A careful man stands always on the side of reason and never that of passion, either because he foresees it from the first, or because he finds it better afterward. When your stand has been anticipated by your adversary, quickly find replacement for your argument or for yourself.

THE NATURAL MAN IS ALWAYS MORE PLEASING

Affectation is the act of taking on an attitude of behavior not natural to oneself. It is as distasteful to everybody else as it is painful to him who practices it, for he is constantly witnessing and agonizing over speech and conduct not natural to himself. The greater your qualifications, the less the need to affect any of them, since all that is natural is always more pleasing than the artificial. The man of confidence and discrimination never flaunts his strength, for it is through its very concealment that it awakens the interest of others. He is twice great who carries all his perfections within himself and avoids the characteristics of conceit.

BE MORE THAN WHAT YOU REPRESENT

What you have to give must exceed the requirements of your office, and not the other way around. For however high may be your post, you must show yourself superior to it in your person. A man of great qualifications tends to grow and to demonstrate this superior talent in his work. But the man who has reached the pinnacle by devious means or faked ability soon reaches the end of his official duties, worse still, the end of his reputation. The genuine leader holds himself greater as a man than the position he holds. Free from hypocrisy and pretense, he truly exceeds the requirements of his office and becomes a star to follow.

KEEP TO THE MIDDLE GROUND

It is well at times to be dependent upon others, so that others may be dependent upon you; thus he who holds a public office must be a public slave, or let him renounce his crown with his cargo. On the other side stand those who belong too completely to others, a case of stupidity going to extremes. Not a day, not even an hour remains their own, bound ever so entirely to others that they have been called "the man for everybody." Therefore, let the man of sense follow the middle ground and take time to care for himself. Let him realize that none is looking out for him and others may only have selfish interest in him, or through him.

LEARN FROM YOUR MISTAKES, THEN LEARN TO FORGET THEM

All men go wrong at times, but with this difference: The intelligent quickly put behind them what they have committed, whereas fools expose even what they may be thinking of committing. It is a mistake to confide your errors even to a friend, for were it possible, you should not disclose them to yourself. Learn from your mistakes, then learn to forget them.

THINK TWICE, SPEAK ONCE

Fickle memory often plays the villain by forsaking us when we need her most, and appearing fresh and eager to please us when we need her least. The former makes us appear dim-witted, the latter foolish for talking too much. The rule is: Think twice, speak once.

EXTREME INDIVIDUALITY CAN DESTROY RESPECT

Either by affectation or through carelessness, extreme individuality is not in the best interests of men seeking respect in public places or industry. The zaniness of their actions is easily regarded as disgrace rather than distinction. Attired in bizarre costumes, as though clowns performing on stage, they will come to be regarded, with their idiosyncrasies, as clowns of another kind: fools and misfits who must rely upon eccentric garb to attract attention. Outlandishness in dress and raucousness in actions offend many, who, with good manners, remain silent. Excessiveness does not serve to make the individual, but only to mark him. For such men it is advised that they play the fool at home, as this offers a greater chance for survival.

BE A MAN OF SUBSTANCE

men in different positions in life have different roles to play. Some play them well, some poorly. The test of a leader is not always determined by success or failure; the greater test is whether he is followed willingly or grudgingly. The wise general knows that praise yields a better soldier. Tact and careful judgment are necessary for subordinates; the frivolous are held in disrespect, for frivolousness stands directly opposed to earnestness. A fool can never prove himself a man of substance, especially an old fool, for his years require that he have an accumulation of good sense, knowledge, and learning. And although this fault of feebleness is the fault of many who reach their winter years, nonetheless it is peculiarly degrading.

THE RICHEST FAILURE IN THE WORLD

There once was a man who was pleased beyond words that he was the owner of the biggest house and the best belongings in the province where he lived. His pompous boastfulness was beyond toleration, but because of his great wealth and because he employed the town's people, none dared confront him. He was not admired, not loved, just used whenever the occasion permitted. In the eyes of many he was considered a pitiful person. How much greater the man would have been had the gifts of his spirit equaled his possessions. Everything is infinite, everything immeasurable in God, and so must everything about a hero be great and majestic. A man of quality and of bearing must be clothed in tasteful thinking, and all his acts, seen or unseen, must transcend the ordinary. Failing this, he is the richest failure in the world.

GRACIÁN'S RECOLLECTIONS

THE EIGHTH ENTRY:

◆

the spanish mind

𝐀 cooler wind from the north brings the first sign of winter into my room. It is invigorating; still, I am having difficulty breathing. The village doctor suggests that I add a mixture of herbs to my teapot so that it becomes some sort of magical witches' brew. But I pay little heed to it all; my mind is locked into the journey of my recollections.

I go back to Zaragoza, 1651, when I was made professor of sacred scriptures, a teaching position I valued greatly. I had just completed a lecture when a student, upon leaving the room, handed me a copy of a just released public notice; I glanced at it and felt a stab of pain jolt through me. The notice read: "ANNOUNCEMENT! ANNOUNCEMENT! The pretentious book, Part One, The Criticizer, by one who falsely calls himself Garcia de Marlones, is hereby banned from the eyes and ears of the public. The possession of this book constitutes a mortal sin and the possessors are subject to loyalty evaluations by the leaders of the Church." Signed: Segovia Montoro, Archbishop, Diocese of Barcelona, January 8, 1651. The day of my fiftieth birthday.

In The Criticizer, planned as a three-volume project, I had intended to create an allegorical vision of human life in the form of letters, dialogue, satire, and fables. I innocently believed that I had received the last of the Archbishop's warnings after King Philip assured me he would speak to His Excellency on my behalf. And now this! Censured! The vindictive Bishop just would not cease hounding me!

I discussed the predicament with Señor de Parada, who advised me to let the banned book find its own way, and to continue writing Part Two of The Criticizer. He assured me that most of the monks and friars, either in need of money or having belief in what I had to say, had promised him that they would continue to turn out copies.

Utilizing every spare minute, I continued writing. But when my eyes burned and my head throbbed, I turned to my wonderful friend, Father Lastanosa. Through our conversations I could escape from the problems of the world that daily loomed larger.

The Inquisition which began under the direction of Ferdinand and Isabella remained a constant embarrassment.

Even today, expulsions are forcing families to live as Roman Catholic while covertly maintaining their traditional beliefs. The wounds of the humiliating defeat of our Spanish Armada are still unhealed. The loss of sixty-eight vessels with more than fifteen thousand young sailors killed or drowned in the English Channel battle with the Dutch was more than a country could bear. And only a few years ago came the concession of independence to the United Provinces; this after nearly a century of wasted war. The results: untold numbers of Roman Catholics are abandoning their churches in protest.

But even in dying, life goes on in Spain. It was at one of my meetings with Father Lastanosa that I was introduced to his cousin, Manuel de Salinas. Señor de Salinas was a serious author, greatly admired even though his works were written in Latin and his readership was limited. When Father Lastanosa was not available, it was Señor de Salinas's company that I eagerly sought.

Our closeness was both gratifying and frustrating. While we admired each other's writings and enjoyed each other's conversations, our views differed. Whereas my work examined virtues and vices and how man could save himself, his work echoed the philosophy of the elders of the Church. Señor de Salinas's view was that these pious churchmen were chosen by God to continue the traditional teachings that brought orderliness to people. My argument was that the world is constantly changing and, as teachers, we owe it to our followers, at whatever levels they may be, to educate them in ways that fit the times.

The difference of opinions continued to the point where

we could no longer be friends. I was saddened by this turn of events, as was Señor de Salinas. When we met now and then, we never spoke about it. Perhaps it was a mistake for us to have gone so deeply into each other's minds.

1652. The first day of the new year began with a visit from Señor de Parada, who cheerfully presented me with the first foreign translation of my work. It was an English edition of The Hero translated by Sir J. Sheffington. The book was magnificently bound. My excitement that day was such that I never inquired how my patron acquired this treasure.

Inwardly aglow at the recognition of my work in a foreign country, I continued writing Part Two of The Criticizer with a new abundance of vigor and inspiration. The world, indeed, was shrinking, and I was becoming part of it.

Contrary to expectation, Part One, though banned, was finding its way into the hands of many readers, just as my sponsor had predicted. Among the people who owned a copy of the book was Calderón de la Barca, the Spanish religious dramatist whom critics often compared with William Shakespeare.

Calderón and I had corresponded previously and had met several times through the years, but one spring day in 1653 the famous man, my book hidden under his cloak, came to call. He had underlined passages of religious crosscurrents that he wished to discuss. Later, when our conversation turned to our beloved Spain, his brow became furrowed and his face expressed despair. It was then that I understood the real nature of his visit: The general disinte-

gration of moral values that marked our era had become unbearably painful to him. He was born into wealth, yet his passion for the common man was heroic.

Calderón de la Barca, who was my age, strongly believed that all who address the public, in any form, are mandated by God to deliver the truth, and he strongly urged that I continue the heart and spirit of my work.

The man knew well about speaking out! He once was jailed for inserting into one of his religious plays criticism of the finger-pointing sermons of a rather arrogant but influential preacher. Having studied law, he was able to extradite himself quickly, and in doing so, made himself famous.

Except for a brief supper in the company of my Jesuit brothers, we spent over six hours conversing, debating, arguing, and finally wondering where the time had gone.

If, prior to my encounter with this astonishing man, I had sinned in the eyes of God and faltered at times in my faith in man, the pride of my heritage was eloquently restored, and my belief in the individual's dignity and worth that day reached exalted heights. I resolved to double my efforts in extending my humanitarian doctrines to all who would listen, to resurrect common sense.

At the expense of my health I was writing long hours into the night. The momentum was such that I could not withdraw.

In rereading the completed chapters I became aware of a recurring theme. I was making a strong argument for the necessity of balance and awareness if one is to build a sensible, meaningful life for himself. I felt that each day called

for a new assessment of events which unfold before our
eyes, and that it is the understanding of certain values that
is the most essential.

The value of living in wholesomeness.
The value of the power to do greater good.
The value of a refreshed spirit.
The value of constant alertness and sustained dignity.
The value of knowing how to plead your case.
The value of judging men by the questions they ask.
The value of not being beholden for everything.
The value of understanding flattery.
The value of not seeking to be loved too much.
The value of understanding the minds of men.
The value of finding the footing to the mountaintop.

With heightened energy I continued writing, from memory, my series of little sermons.

THE ORACLE

Gracián On:

Balance and Awareness

THE MORE MATURITY, THE MORE THE MAN

maturity gives radiance to your person and to your persona. As material weight multiplies the value of gold, moral weight increases your worth as a man; it is the reason for respect, and the grounds for veneration. Maturity is the heightened preparedness for all challenges in the adult world. The enlightened man knows that his composure is the facade of his spirit; it speaks with authority or uncertainty, with serenity or anxiety, with finality or inquiry. The more maturity, the more the man. You cease being a child when you begin to mature and carry authority.

STAY ON THE ALERT

Fate likes to play the spoiler and upset the best of plans in order to catch the sleeper. Be aware. Always stand ready for inspection in spirit, in mind, in fortitude, even in appearance, for the day that these are left to themselves becomes the day of downfall. Alertness is always essential, for to be without it slates one for possible destruction of mind and/or body. It has always been the strategy of certain men to challenge your qualifications by rigorous inspection when your guard is down. The day for the parade is already known, but it is on the day least expected that the soldier is reviewed for the severest test.

Seek to overcome shortcomings

many would be counted as great persons were it not for a few shortcomings; it is as though the top of the mountain is visible to them but they cannot find their footing. When observing certain men, it becomes obvious that they have the potential to be something more, if they could only repair small failings. Some lack earnestness, which blurs their great gifts. Others lack friendliness of disposition. In men on the rise, these faults are noticed all too quickly by those about them. Insincerity, temper, greed, lack of truth-telling, all these frailties, if they were given attention, could easily be overcome.

MAKE YOUR WORDS COUNT

Train yourself to hold the interest of one or many. Since you are judged by the depth of your questions and the ideas you affirm, it is to your credit to express the uncommon and forgo the banal.

CATCH THE TRUE MEANING IN OTHERS' WORDS

Do not hold in too high opinion the man who never opposes you in cross conversation, for that is not a token of love for you, but of love for himself. Neither allow yourself to be deceived through flattery, nor to be pleased by it. Instead, reason the real purpose of flowery speeches implanted in your ears. Some men cleverly offer all you want to hear. Beware, for they are the ones with the gift of making falsehood sound like truth. Keep in mind that some men speak against you. You will know who they are when, in your presence, they speak ill of others.

PREPARE YOURSELF FOR ADVERSITY

In good times prepare yourself for the bad. Learn from the animals who spend much of their time gathering food in autumn to nourish them through the winter. In times of good fortune friends are plentiful, favors come easily. Store all that is necessary in preparation for adversity, a time when all things fail. Keep careful records in mind of those men beholden to you, for some day you may welcome those who can be called on to contribute to your cause. There are individuals so independent that they have no real friends in their circle of affluence. When, in times of good fortune, you do not give recognition to good men, in misfortune you will be but another stranger in the crowd.

KNOWING MEN DIFFERS FROM KNOWING MERCHANDISE

The world of business is a place set apart where men deliberately deceive each other. When embarking in business, it is as important to have studied men as to have studied books, for one can easily be seduced by charm and politeness; these are the worst and the easiest of deceptions. A great science it is to understand the minds of men and to discern their humors. There is a difference between knowing merchandise and knowing men, for it is far better to be cheated in the price than in the goods.

CONTRIBUTE TO THE SEVEN-YEAR RENEWAL

Once in every seven years, so it is said, we are made over. During the first seven years intelligence enters. With each succeeding seven, let some new virtue shine forth. Take note of this natural cycle, forever looking toward improvement, in order to help it along. By conducting themselves in this manner many have made great changes in their social status or life's work. Learn how to refresh the spirit through nature and through art. Add wisdom and understanding and patience and forgiveness to each segment of your life if you would elevate and realize your spirit.

Keep obligations to a minimum

Incur the fewest obligations by seeking the fewest favors. Being beholden for everything or to everyone is to become the property of another, both controlled and influenced. Independence is more precious than any gift you may give up for it. A favor of personal gratification often leads to indebtedness beyond your desire. More satisfying, by far, is that many depend upon you. This is a source of power. And the power to command has only one advantage: the power to do greater good. But be most careful not to mistake an obligation put upon you as a favor, because usually the other's astuteness has managed to make it so appear. Having someone grant you authority might reward your ego, but not necessarily reward your effort.

APPRECIATION IS BETTER THAN DEVOTION

For a man positioned for advancement, even greatness, it is better to be regarded by his constituents appreciatively rather than devotedly. Affection ushers in familiarity, and for every step it might take forward, it is likely that it will move one back as well. It is a rare joy to couple devotion and respect, but if you would maintain the respect in which you are held be not loved too much, nor feared too much. Love is both sensitive and bold and, because of this dichotomy, can quickly turn to hate. Affection and deep reverence do not always marry well because they are so thinly bound. Your position is best held together by outside recognition of quality and value over warmth and gentleness.

EVEN IN PARADISE IT IS NOT GOOD TO BE ALONE

For the most part, it is better to go with the crowd and be considered ordinary than to be endowed with a world of wisdom and be alone. For this reason, at times the greatest knowledge is to know nothing, or to affect to know nothing. It has been said that even in paradise, it is not good to be alone, that too much aloneness saps the spirit. To live a balanced life, it is sensible to be admitted to the life-styles of many. Observing the mistakes of others is an easier learning experience than benefiting from your own, though both are necessary. In this world we have little choice but to live with others, though the dull and crass make up the majority. To live alone one must have within himself either much of God, or much of the jungle beast.

BE SLOW TO BELIEVE

It is wise to defer judgment on most matters, especially those of consequence. Be not too quickly convinced; it is a sign of immaturity. Maturity is best displayed in the deliberateness with which a man adopts even his own beliefs. Be slow to believe, and slow to cherish. Instant allegiance indicates a lack of discretion, for many exaggerate and lie in word, as they lie in deed, and the latter is more deadly because it is set in motion. At the same time, do not exhibit your immediate doubt in the faith of another, for that passes as discourtesy or even insult. Know that the false is the ordinary of the day. Let what you believe in be the carefully measured extraordinary.

PLACE LEISURE AFTER LABOR

If you would be acknowledged as a man of good sense, place leisure *after* labor. The essential should come first, and then, if opportunity is left, the secondary. Some take to relaxation at the day's beginning and leave labor for its end. Others seek to triumph before they have battled. Many begin by study of the trivial, postponing, until the evening of life, those studies that might bring them fame and success in their prime. Another has not yet begun to climb toward fortune when he goes dizzy. Whereas in youth position is nonexistent, in the adult world it becomes a man's dignity or embarrassment.

DO NOT GO AGAINST THE GRAIN

*T*here are countless roads that lead to a successful life, and most men choose their way led by the voice of their instincts. For the greedy and the imposter, it is the path of trickery; for the principled, it is the straight and narrow. Know, then, how to deal with situations; choose not to go against the grain, even though it may present itself to you that way. Everything has its cutting edge and its blunt edge. The best and most useful of tools, if seized by the blade, wounds; while the most destructive, if grasped by the hilt, protects. Much that has given pain, when taken another way, would have given pleasure, for there is pleasure or pain in everything, and wisdom lies in seeing them in different lights. Discern what is good and what is bad; some discover satisfaction in everything, and others discover only grief. This is the best defense against the reverses of fortune, a master rule of life that at all times is simply this: Look upon everything in its happiest light.

GRACIÁN'S RECOLLECTIONS

THE NINTH ENTRY:

◆

the late evening of my life

J am tired this morning. Extremely tired. I am failing in strength and my pen moves slowly and haltingly. Yet, I am clear in mind, and for this I thank God. This may well be the last day to set my memories free.

During the night, in a vision, I was enveloped in an enormous white cloud. Suddenly a shaft of sunlight laced with crossbars appeared, and on these I ascended in weightless movements. I could hear the silence, and I had the sense that my body was being pulled skyward. My breath came in short gasps. Tears filled my eyes. It was an overwhelming, out-of-body experience such as I have never had before.

This morning I think back to the year 1654. My professorship in Zaragoza was going well. Had I not been in a position to aid a fellow writer, a most important anthology of poetry would have been wasted. José Alfay's Collection of Great Spanish Poets was a compilation of poems from writers whose ideas linked them to the moral thinking of the times. This collection of poetry was so cleverly crafted that it was quite difficult to grasp whether the writers were being diplomatic and incisive, or were merely mocking the establishment.

In his anthology Alfay captured the misery of the nation, and because we were observed together I was brought to task by my superiors and accused of having a hand in the completion of his work. In fact, I was accused of having written the fiery prologue that was the basis of the vital issues behind the poetry. This was not true. My only involvement with the work was in admiring it and bringing it to the attention of my benefactor, Señor de Parada, who, upon reading the brilliantly conceived work, raised the needed money to have the book published.

Alfay's anthology became enormously successful, but my good friend, Pablo de Parada, did not participate in its victory. Soon after his involvement with the Collection of Great Spanish Poets, he was thrown from a horse and died in-

stantly. Hundreds of mourners, people he had never met, attended his funeral.

I was informed that the rumor of my association with this book of provocative poetry had reached the ears of the palace, and so I was not surprised when, shortly afterward, a messenger arrived with a handwritten note from King Philip IV addressed to me. However, the contents of the note did surprise me. It contained a single sentence: "Father Gracián is cordially invited to celebrate morning mass in the chapel of the palace this Sunday, 12th April, at nine o'clock." Signed, Philip IV.

Later, when I questioned Father Lastanosa about the urgency of the invitation, the good Father replied: "Baltasar, you are so naive. You are a celebrity. The king is curious to see and hear for himself why your Sunday masses are filled to the rafters. There is nothing more to it." He then added: "Incidentally, I hear that royalty is visiting the palace."

On arriving at the palace gate that Sunday morning, I was met by an escort who led me to the front of the chapel. Promptly at nine o'clock I proceeded to the altar, and after the gospel I mounted the pulpit, my heart beating wildly. I recognized King Philip in a side room, half hidden by a heavy curtain. A man of regal appearance sat next to him.

This was the highlight of my life, the oppportunity to address His Majesty, to conduct a traditional service and afterward, in my sermon, to open a vein that led to the heart of my frustrations. With one voice I could speak for millions of my countrymen.

I stood in the pulpit for almost an hour, and from the moment my first word was uttered I could feel a rush of fire surging through my body. My trembling voice rose and fell, demanding the full attention of every person there. Lost in the passion of the moment, I found myself expanding my sermon to include the ills of the world, and here in my beloved Spain, the plight of good men being caught in constant struggle, and the moral disintegration that inevitably followed.

The darkness that had filled my years prompted perhaps the bleakest commentary that ever poured from the depths of my heart. I remember well how I concluded my sermon that Sunday morning:

> *All that exists makes sport of miserable Man: the world tricks him, life lies to him, fate mocks him, age depresses him, health fails him, evil hastens him, good avoids him, the years flee, contentment never arrives, life ends, death grabs him, the grave consumes him, the earth covers him, rotting decays him, oblivion annihilates him, and he who was man yesterday, today is dust and tomorrow nothing.*

Then, exhausted, my body drenched in perspiration, I adjourned to an anteroom, poured myself a cup of water, and closed my eyes. When I opened them again there stood Philip along with an ornately dressed man with massive, wavy hair flowing down to his shoulders. There was no introduction. The king's only remarks were: "Gracián, you were superb. I suppose you will never learn." The other gentleman, speaking French, respectfully questioned me on aspects of education, always beginning with "Father, what are your thoughts on this . . . that?" And it went on.

In a short while they were gone. In their place appeared an elderly Jesuit who was assigned to escort me to the carriage for my return journey.

Glancing about to assure himself that he could not be heard, the Jesuit clutched my arm as we walked through the square, and with his stare fixed straight ahead, whispered: "Father Gracián, your sermon was magnificent." He looked over his shoulder. "The regal gentleman with Philip, do you know who he is?" And without waiting for a reply he continued: "The King. Louis. King Louis XIV of France. While the nations are warring, the monarchs are dining!"

Indeed, it was a day unlike any other day in my life. Exhilarating. Exhausting. Frightening. And on this chilly December morning as I look back on my life, I see that, as a whole, it was also at turns exhilarating, exhausting, frightening. Indeed my fatigue today seems intensified, although I am strangely at peace. Thank God the work is nearly finished.

In retrospect, my allotted time on earth did not coincide with the glorious days of Spain. On the other hand, my time may have been divinely chosen.

If my obsession to inspire the common man to be less common did not turn out well in the eyes of others, I must then assume that what they observed they did not see clearly. Surely there will be others in the future who will understand my motives. I pray that these clear-thinking men may become great leaders, and with selflessness and kindness help the less fortunate to a better life. Just as I have allowed ideas to use me—and there is no other way for an idea to survive—I pray my own writings will use them to educate and inspire those who wish to listen.

In the end, the Bishop—what an enigma he is!—will have his complete revenge. He has won the last battle which was precipitated by the publication of the third and final part of The Criticizer, *the money having been left by Señor de Parada for this purpose. Not only have I been exiled and my works confiscated, but soon I will be no more.*

The Bishop's private war against those who speak out will not end with my departure. Does he not know that there will always be a procession of enlightened and outspoken men? Does he not know that the flame of free thought is not easily extinguished?

The Bishop will not have me to contend with, but in my place will be a more formidable foe. It will be the words I leave behind.

To assure myself that my restated work will not be impounded, I have a plan. It is a simple one. I will prepare two signed and witnessed documents, one for Calderon de la Barca, and the other for Archbishop Segovia Montoro. After my death, these documents, along with the completed manuscript of The Oracle, *will be delivered by Senor and Senora Blanca to Calderon. As prearranged, my clever playwriting friend will carry out two errands. He will see that the Archbishop receives the document addressed to his Excellency, and he will place the manuscript in the custody of my dear and trusted friend, Vincencio Lastanosa, publisher of several of my previous works.*

The witnessed document to Archbishop Montoro will contain my departing message. It will read:

I, BALTASAR GRACIÁN, WITH SOUND MIND
AND CLEAR PURPOSE, UNCONDITIONALLY,
AND WITH DEEP REVERENCE, BEQUEATH THE
FULL EMBODIMENT OF The Oracle *TO ALMIGHTY*
GOD, AND TO THE WINDS OF TIME.
(Signed) Father Baltasar Gracián, 2nd December 1658

I am at peace with myself knowing that these writings of my heart and soul cannot be wrested from God. They will return from whence they came. They evermore will belong to the Creator of all things.

And when I commence my return from whence I came, I will take leave with eternal love for all who shared with me my days on earth, and with complete forgiveness in my heart for His Excellency, Archbishop Segovia Montoro, who, for reasons that I shall never know, chose to be my enemy.

The Oracle is dedicated to Man, who, at one with God, is worthy to survive, to grow, to learn, so that he can make a difference in the world.

I rest now, in order to complete the last of my work.

THE ORACLE

Gracián On:

WINNING WAYS

WHAT IS INDIGESTION TO ONE IS ONLY APPETITE TO ANOTHER

The capacity to digest large slices of good fortune leads to bigger slices, for he who is worthy of more will not be gorged. What is indigestion to one is only appetite to another. There are many who will turn sick whenever the gamble is high because they are naturally weak, being neither accustomed to nor born to prosperity. The undertaking sours on them, and from the fumes arising out of their unearned distinction, they appear unsteady. Others, observing this, soon retreat from much to do with them in the future. There are risks for those unable to maintain themselves in high places. Therefore, let the capable man show evidence that he has the capacity for even larger enterprise, and above all, let him avoid anything that suggests weakness.

LESS SMART, MORE WISE

Showing how smart you are plays into the hands of enemies and critics. It is more important to be wise. To display too much edge is to go dull, for what is too pointed commonly breaks off. We are all smart at some things, not all things, and dumb at others, and we like to believe that our unique intelligence is more important than that of others. Most secure is a life of ordained truth. It is well to have fine brains, but not a babbling tongue, for too much discourse borders on dispute. A good level judgment does not wander afield more than is necessary.

GOODWILL IS THE REPAYMENT OF A MAN'S INTEGRITY

Goodwill is one of the great assets of mankind and is available to both rich and poor for the price of charm; it is the repayment of a man's integrity. Goodwill's value to an enterprise goes beyond the mere worth of what it sells; it is so great that goodwill can be sold by itself. Some have such faith in its value that they hold perseverance ordinary by comparison. A man alert in the ways of the world knows well that the path of mere merit is a stony one if he is not helped by the approval and support of others. Unless goodwill is dissipated, the man who wears this mantle is rarely scrutinized for shortcomings, because the observer does not wish to see them. Such is the power of goodwill and it should be known.

Develop a sophisticated manner

Being distinctively different in speech and in action suggests style and superiority. It can dazzle and at best it makes a large place for itself everywhere and compels respect in advance. Sophistication shows itself in everything, in bearing, in talk, at times in the walk, or even in the look, and in the desire to succeed. A great victory it is to win the hearts of rivals, especially when it is accomplished by the ways of the man who is elegantly set apart from the ordinary.

MAKE SURE YOUR ACCOMPLISHMENTS CAN BE SEEN

Do, and have what you do be noticed, because things do not pass only for what they are but also for what they seem. To have achieved value, and to know how to show it, is to be twice favored. A man is valued as he esteems himself. For those you wish to impress, the rule is: That which is not made apparent does not exist. Even good is not respected if it does not look good. Many observers are taken in by their own perception, and the gullible far outnumber the smart. Today hoax, tricks, and illusion often rule, and things are judged quickly and carelessly, not as in the past when there was time for all things. If you would have your accomplishments acknowledged, make sure they can be seen.

THE ART OF CONVERSATION IS THE HALLMARK OF THE MAN

Some believe that conversation at work should be informal, like the clothing we wear on our days of rest. This may hold true between friends, but where it is to gain respect, conversation must have form to better display the substance of who you are. The art of conversation is the hallmark of the man, and no human enterprise demands greater care. If care is necessary in order to write a letter, which is edited coversation committed to paper, how much more is necessary in everyday speech when the intelligence must at every moment pass examination! Men skilled in oratory are able to take the pulse of the soul and place it on the tongue. In verbal exchange, to strike it right you must be able to adapt yourself to the spirit of your company. Do not make yourself a critic of words or you will be held the grammatical fool; nor the opponent of what is reasonable or all men will look doubtfully upon what you have to say. Discretion in what is said is far better than eloquence, for a word once spoken is an arrow let fly.

AT TIMES BE NOT TOO CLEAR IN ORDER NOT TO SEEM TOO ORDINARY

Be able to express yourself not only clearly but with charm. Some speakers offer considerable information but fall short in delivery. Others pour forth more than anticipated. The latter tends to confuse because the concept of the subject was not properly explained at the start. What resolution is to the will, exposition is to the mind, and both are great attributes. Clear heads are praised, but those considered confused may be respected as well, because they are not understood and are presumed to be intelligent. The decoration of charm and enchantment to one's speech lends it a degree of mysticism even if it is without sound basis. At times be not too clear in order not to seem too ordinary.

SUPPORT YOUR WORDS WITH DEEDS

*T*he consummate man, polished and masterful in the eyes of his peers, is the one who will voice what is good and do what is honorable. Such actions are evidence of a good head and a kind heart, and together they beget a great soul. Seeing the good in a bad situation enhances the character of the person, and can escalate him to uncommon heights in a society where pointing out the bad is commonplace. Achievement is the substance of life, and praise its decoration. Greatness only in words is ephemeral and confirms the shallowness of the speaker. Support of words by deeds is honorable; thus greatness in action endures.

CIVILITY IS A SUBTLE CONQUEROR

most men neither speak nor act in the true sense of what they are, but as they must. Driven by the need to win, they enter into wrongdoing; they engage in slander, which is easily believed by others, however unbelievable. Yet the most and best of what a man is resides in the opinion of others. Some rest content because right is on their side; but this is not enough, for it needs the help of good form. If good reputation concerns a man, he will understand that to be obliging usually costs little, yet is worth much. For with mere words, he buys deeds. Respect inspires respect. Civility, the refinement of good breeding, is the subtle conqueror of all.

SENSE THE MOOD OF THOSE AROUND YOU

Do not fail to catch the other's mood, lest you give him pain instead of pleasure. Recognize the spirit of the moment and embrace it, for words that flatter one may offend another, and what is intended as a compliment becomes a provocation. It has often cost more to make a man unhappy than it would have cost to make him happy. His gratitude can easily be lost because the guiding star to his pleasure was not seen. When you do not sense another's mood it is difficult to sustain a dialogue, for it is then that conversations take the wrong turn and lead to nothingness. In trying to voice praise, one's words may land on deaf ears, and in trying to charm by eloquence, you may only bruise the spirit by talkativeness.

SUGARCOAT YOUR WORDS

As thorns pierce the body, so hard words wound the soul. Always carry a mouthful of sugar so that your sweetened speech will please even your enemies. Most things are paid for in words, and sweetened words suffice to discharge the impossible debt. For the only way to be loved is to be amiable. Heavenly affairs are done with the heavens and life-giving words give life. Honey-coated words dulcify the favor asked, just as indulging in a good cake sweetens the breath. The scent of nectar is sensed by many, but to be effective and not offensive the request must be sprinkled with sincerity.

COURTESY IS LIKE SORCERY

Good manners are made up of little sacrifices. Courtesy is the stem of culture, and like sorcery, wins the affection of everyone. Gain the reputation of being a gentleman, for this good name is enough to make you loved, just as discourtesy gathers scorn and makes you hated. When discourtesy is born of arrogance, it is abominable; when of coarseness, detestable. One can count on unexpected dividends from acts of courtesy even in dealing with enemies, for it exhibits courage, and the cost is little. Bravery and courtesy have this advantage: They are saved through being spent. Give in abundance of either and it still remains with you.

DEVELOP A REPUTATION FOR CHARM

Charm is everything. It is a gift of nature and owes little to schooling, to which, in fact, it is superior. It is the life of the talents, the flower of speech, the soul of action, the halo of splendor itself. It is the simplest weapon, yet the most potent. It is a thing of ease, yet approaches daring; it takes the difficulty out of conversation and adds perfection to performance. Without charm beauty is meaningless, and all grace, graceless, for this formidable trait transcends courage, wisdom, reason, and greatness itself. Charm is the courteous way to get about in every enterprise, and the polite way to wriggle out of every embarrassment.

LET EACH MAN, IN HIS WAY, BE MAJESTIC ACCORDING TO HIS STATION

Aspire to be markedly superior in character and quality. Strive for growth in mind and spirit, for spirit, the vital spark within all physical lives, is needed for balance. Let each man, in his way, be majestic according to his station, and his ways be regal within the limits of his gifts. Greatness in action and loftiness of mind in everything he does are the true mark of the leader, and rarely are these characteristics bestowed upon him by birth. The leader with sovereign qualities is the prototype of the best who preceded him. He did not merely assume the attributes and grow pompous, but he let them become productive within him. It is said that no man need envy greatness if he is an example of it.

TALENT OUTSHINES POSITION

If you would be considered important, let it be through the excellence of your talents rather than through your high position. For even a king should be worshiped more because of his qualifications than because of the accident of his birth. Those who attain genuine importance are seldom the ones who make a show of what they have. It is offensive to boast of your status; for to make yourself the central figure is to make yourself envied. If you prize praise you must also be ready to experience resentment. Those who heavily trade upon the importance of their office show that they themselves are not noble enough for the honor. Respect depends upon others. One cannot claim it or snatch it, but only deserve it, and wait.

THE TRIUMPH OVER ENVY

Whereas leadership is recognized by victories, there is another victory recognized only by oneself. It is the triumph over envy. It is the greatest of self-punishments to be made unhappy by another's happiness, bearing out that men always hate most what they envy most. No man shall ever be enriched by envy.

DISARM YOUR OPPONENTS WITH GOODWILL

There are men who when holding the cards of advantage play with reckless abandon. They use all their skill in discharging innuendos to torment their opponent. It is not enough to ignore those who would speak against you; better to meet them with energetic handshake and smiling face. There is not enough praise for you if you speak well of him who speaks ill of you.

SEIZE THAT ONE GREAT MOMENT THAT WILL LIGHT UP YOUR SKY

We are born, all of us, with at least one special talent, one skill to hone to perfection with the passage of time. This gift must be registered early, in anticipation of that one great moment of opportunity that will light up our sky. Seize it, for not every day will be triumphant! Fortunately, there are moments of smaller degree in which to display natural endowments. Expose these talents, much like the merchant who exhibits wares to attract buyers. It was light that first revealed the whole of creation, and it was exposition that gave life to everything. Even that which is most excellent leans upon its surroundings. But there is a caveat! Exposition, closely tied to vanity, easily turns into ostentation. It flirts with cheapness and often fares badly. Don't exhibit all you have at once, but allow frequent glimpses, always bringing forward more. Each accomplishment must carry the pledge of another and a greater, and in this way the applause will increase.

THE HAPPY ENDING

In the minds of many there is a heaven and a hell. The earth upon which we live lies somewhere in the middle. We live between the two extremes, and so partake of both, be it great happiness or adversity. It is said that by itself the world is nothing but, joined to heaven and hell, is everything. The adoration of one and the fear of the other shapes our being, and we grow expedient. We learn that acceptance of our lot in life is common sense, and to not be surprised by it is wisdom. Our life becomes more complicated as we go along, but toward its end it becomes simpler, much like reaching the mountain summit where the downward trek to the valley awaits us. If we keep our balance throughout the journey, we eventually stumble into the happy ending.

Baltasar Gracián

died on

December 6, 1658,

In Tarragona

Books by Baltasar Gracián

The Hero (El héroe) 1637

✦

The Politician (El politico) 1640

✦

Wit and the Art of Ingenuity (Agudeza y arte de ingenio) 1642

✦

The Discreet Man (El discreto) 1646

✦

The Manual Oracle and the Art of Prudence (Oraculo Manual y Arte de Prudencia) 1647

✦

The Communion Rail (El comulgatorio) 1655

✦

The Criticizer (El criticón) 1651, 1653, 1657